THESE STRANGE GERMAN WAYS

ATLANTIK-BRÜCKE E.V.

Adenauerallee 131, D-5300 Bonn 1
Tel.: 02 28 / 21 41 60
Telex: 8869307 abbn d

The "Atlantic Bridge" is encharged by its bylaws with increasing understanding of Germany in the United States, as well as of the United States in Germany, and thus contributing to German-American friendship. The organization seeks to advance this goal in a variety of ways. It is particularly concerned with encouraging and arranging direct German-American contacts in both German and American political, economic and cultural centers. It also seeks to inform the public with occasional publications. In addition, the organization works with similarly-interested groups and individuals on cooperative projects.

Sixteenth Edition

Published by Atlantik-Brücke e. V.
Heschredder 52, 2000 Hamburg 63, Federal Republic of Germany

Picture Series and Cover by Jörn

Printed in Germany by Wullenwever-Druck Heine KG, Lübeck

All rights reserved

ISBN 3-925744-07-X

Cover Photo:
Carnival in Cologne
Michael Engler/Bilderberg

A Word About This Booklet

"These Strange German Ways!" — how many a visitor to Germany, confounded by different manners and customs, might have uttered this complaint? The *Atlantik-Brücke*, a private West German organization dedicated to bridging the gap between Germans and Americans, took this complaint seriously. It began to explain these strange German ways, first in a series of cartoons in *The Bridge*, a monthly paper published for American servicemen stationed in Germany, later in a separate publication.

These Strange German Ways proved to be a success far beyond original expectations. Apparently it filled a need, not only for American servicemen and their families, but also for other English-speaking visitors to Germany. Since 1963, 16 editions have been published. Along the way, its contents have been revised repeatedly. Customs were changing rapidly along with the West Germans' way of life, which by now closely resembles the life style of other Western industrialized countries. Today, West Germany just does not seem to be that "strange" a country anymore. Yet the continued demand for *These Strange German Ways* indicates that there is still a need to explain its peculiar habits and customs to our visitors and guests from abroad. Superficially, the differences might no longer appear to be all that pronounced. But it is often the little misunderstandings that lead to irritations, disappointments, or even culture shock. This booklet is intended to help avoid such misunderstandings and make things a little easier for the newcomer.

We are grateful to all those who have contributed to *These Strange German Ways* with valuable tips and suggestions. Pride of place must be given to Adolph Schalk, an American writer and newspaperman, who created *The Bridge* and began the series on "These Strange German Ways". Other contributors were Carolyn Campbell, Jürgen Brandes, Ruth M. Irvin, Robert C. Larson, Victor Baras, Joetta Moltmann, Marian Tursich, Hans Dolezalek, Harry Davis, Heide Wyse, Billie Ann Lopez, and Evelyn Schultes. For several useful tips and ideas we are indebted to the American Women's Club of Hamburg.

Great care has been taken to make sure that all facts and figures are correct and up to date. Nevertheless, some errors may have escaped us and some details may have become obsolete after publication. The editor is grateful for any inaccuracies brought to her attention for revision in the next edition. *These Strange German Ways* should not be any stranger than they already are.

Beate Lindemann

Vice Chairman and Program Director
Atlantik-Brücke e. V.

Irmgard Burmeister

Editor

Table of Contents

The Social Courtesies

Most Americans in Germany know that *Auf Wiedersehen* means "good-bye". But what is *Tschüss?* And *Grüss Gott?* And what do the Germans say for "thank you", for "how are you", and for "excuse me"?

Even if you don't speak the language, knowing a few words of greeting, of thanks, of apology, will make you feel so much better in the foreign surroundings. And knowing some basic differences in the social courtesies — when to shake hands, when to use first names, how to introduce people — can make all the difference.

Try it and see!

Very Glad To Meet You!

"Darf ich bekannt machen?
Herr Meier — Frau Schmidt."
"Guten Abend, Frau Schmidt!"
"Guten Abend, Herr Meier!"
(Don't say, "Wie geht es Ihnen")

What do you say when introducing people to each other in Germany? Say *"Darf ich bekannt machen?"* or *"Darf ich vorstellen? — Herr Meier — Frau Schmidt"*. The two shake hands, smile and say *"Guten Abend (Guten Tag), Herr/Frau . . ."* to each other. A friendly nod of the head when shaking hands would do, too. You may also say *"Freut mich sehr"* or *"sehr angenehm"* (corresponding to the American "Very glad to meet you") on such occasions, but these phrases are regarded as somewhat old-fashioned by many Germans and not used much anymore.

Americans, who are used to saying "How do you do" or "how are you" when being introduced, may be tempted to say *"Wie geht es Ihnen?"* when being introduced to a German. This, however, is not customary. *"Wie geht es Ihnen"* is a greeting for someone you already know, and when using it be prepared to get a detailed answer. Even the more casual *"Wie geht's?"* may be understood as an inquiry rather than a polite greeting. *"Danke, gut!"* (thank you, fine) would be the normal answer, though.

As a rule, Germans will prefer being introduced to a stranger by a third person instead of introducing themselves. However, if the circumstances call for it, it is perfectly all right to introduce oneself. Just say your last name: "Schmidt".

And keep in mind: in formal German introductions, the name of the man or, if it concerns two men or two women, the name of the younger or lower ranking person is said first!

Guten Tag! Auf Wiedersehen!

Guten Tag! Guten Morgen! Grüß Gott!

Auf Wiedersehen!

"Hello" or "Hi" have become almost international greetings these days, and many Germans will use them when dealing with Americans. Young people and children in Germany also say *Hallo* now among each other and occasionally when addressing adults.

Otherwise, the normal greeting is *Guten Tag (Abend, Morgen)*. Often, people just mumble *n'Tag, n'Abend,* or *Morgen*. In South Germany, particularly in Bavaria, you often hear *Grüss Gott,* or the informal *Servus* or *Grüss Dich*.

(Auf) Wiedersehen means good-bye. *Tschüss* (originating from the French "A Dieu") is a very casual, primarily North German, form of *Wiedersehen*. It comes closest to the American "See you" or "So long". *Ade* (with the stress on the e) is the Swabian version.

If a German says *bis bald* (until soon) or *bis dann* (until then), he usually has a specific time in mind, something he has just talked about. Actually, there is no need for a German to express his hope to see the other person again, as *Auf Wiedersehen* means exactly that.

Who Shakes Whose Hand?

Germans have a reputation as great hand-shakers. Indeed, they used to pump each others' hands not only when being introduced but also as a normal part of everyday greetings, meaning little more than saying hello.

This, as so many features of a less hectic way of life, has changed rapidly in the last decades. Many Germans shake hands now only when meeting strangers, when seeing friends or relatives after a prolonged absence, or when congratulating. When in doubt whether a handshake is in place, the foreigner would be better off waiting for the German to make the first move.

According to formal convention, it is the senior or the woman who offers the hand first, but this rule, too, is increasingly being ignored. It is considered very bad manners, however, to leave one hand in your pocket when shaking hands.

At a small German party everybody will greet everybody else with a handshake, beginning with the host and hostess. A stranger normally waits until the host makes the introductions. A woman need not rise when greeting a man or another woman, unless the other woman is considerably older or a very distinguished person. A man should rise when a woman enters the room for the first time, but not all men sitting at a table need to rise when a woman is getting up.

When meeting acquaintances in the street, in shops or elsewhere in public, Germans usually shake hands only if they intend to stop and have a little chat.

Sometimes, when two couples greet each other, one can watch a funny little scene: they all stretch out their hands at once and, noticing this, suddenly draw them back before contact, smiling a little wryly. The reason for this is the superstition that one should never shake hands crosswise, as this surely will bring bad luck. The solution to the problem is simple: Ladies first!

Perhaps to make up for less handshaking, Americans do a lot more kissing when greeting each other than Germans. Of late, however, a peck on the cheek among friends is seen more often in Germany than ever before.

The Hand Kiss — Most Men Dislike It

Americans are often startled when witnessing for the first time an old formality of German society — the hand kiss. A survey revealed that about 40 per cent of the German women like this custom, but 80 per cent of the German men don't! By the way: the hand is not actually kissed — a paper-thin sheet of air must remain between the hand and lips. A hand kiss normally takes place indoors, not on the street.

And here's another warning to people not used to hand-kissing: to perform a hand kiss elegantly takes a certain amount of practice, and it fits only on certain occasions. If in doubt, it may be best to simply shake hands.

Too Little Is Better Than Too Much

Only at small parties, family reunions, etc., do all people shake hands, not at large affairs or receptions.

No need to shake hands in the street — unless you are stopping to chat.

The hand kiss is still a custom in formal German society — but the hand is not actually kissed.

More Little Courtesies

Knicks

Compliment

Few German mothers still teach their little daughters to courtsey (einen Knicks machen) when greeting adults. If little boys bow to adults, this is called "einen Diener machen", but this, too, has become a very rare sight.

Don't be surprised if a German girl does not automatically say "thank you" when you have paid her a compliment. She may say "danke schön", but this is not a standard answer as it would be in the States.
The German girl's reply is left more or less up to her imagination.

Bitte schön! Danke sehr! Verzeihung!

Americans sometimes are confused by the many *"Bitte schöns"* and *"Danke sehrs"* that Germans (polite ones, that is) use in their everyday dealings. Here are the basic rules:

If Germans give others something — or if they pick something up for another person, hold the door open, etc. — they often say *"Bitte"* (Bitte sehr, bitte schön).

On receiving something from another person, they will say *"Danke"* (Danke sehr, Danke schön). Upon this, an American might answer "You're welcome". The German answer to *Danke* is *Bitte*, also *nichts zu danken* or *keine Ursache*.

If you step on somebody's foot or bump into someone, what do you say to express that you are sorry? You may say *"Verzeihung"* (Verzeihen Sie, bitte; Entschuldigung; Entschuldigen Sie, bitte). The victim will answer *"Bitte"* or *"Bitte sehr"*.

What do you say if you wish to make your way through a crowd in a bus, streetcar, etc.? The most polite way is to ask, *"Gestatten Sie, bitte?"* but you may also say, *"Entschuldigung, steigen Sie auch aus?"* (are you also getting out?)

Bitte schön! — Danke!

It's easy in this case (ladies first), but if two men or two women want to go through a door, they often make quite a polite fuss over who should go first: "Nach Ihnen!" (after you).

Entschuldigen Sie bitte!

Bitte sehr!

Gnädige Frau — Ihre Gattin — mein Mann

How would the hotel reception clerk address the female guest? Probably with "Gnädige Frau". This is the most polite form of addressing a woman in Germany, comparable in a way to "Madam" in English, although "Gnädige Frau" is more formal.

Suppose these two men know each other only slightly. In asking how the other's wife is doing, they have three grades of formality to choose from: "Wie geht es Ihrer Frau" (normal, but a bit informal), "...Ihrer Gattin" (very polite), "...Ihrer Frau Gemahlin" (very formal).

Speaking of her husband, a woman uses the term "mein Mann". Germans always say "mein Mann" or "meine Frau", no matter how formal the occasion may be.

Is the Fräulein Gone Forever?

In Germany, unmarried adult women are today called *Frau* instead of the former *Fräulein*. The latter is now used only for very young unmarried girls. Woman artists, actresses, or anyone who is distinguished in any way, and who in English usage would be addressed with "Miss", would be called *Frau* (with their family name). In postal addresses, *Frau* is used almost exclusively now. An equivalent to "Ms" does not exist.

Married women are not addressed with their husband's first name — their own first name is used. Thus, it is not "Frau Hans Müller" but "Frau Helga Müller".

Widowed women keep their married name, while divorced women are free to use their maiden name again.

Today, partners in marriage may also choose the woman's name for the family — but very few couples do so, or they use both names.

Wedding Rings

As in many other countries of the Western World, German couples now often live together before marriage. Once married, German wives — contrary to their husbands — prefer to show their marital status: According to a survey made a few years ago, only half of all married men but seven out of eight married women in Germany wear their wedding ring.

Traditionally, Germans wear the wedding ring on the right hand and the engagement ring on the left hand (the engagement ring is usually the same plain gold band that later serves as the wedding ring). Today, however, many men and women wear the wedding ring on the left hand, and only half of all engaged people in Germany wear an engagement ring at all. If an engagement ring is worn, both the woman and the man wear one. — Still others wear a wedding ring without being married. . .

A confusing picture — but it shows clearly the degree to which old-established social rules and attitudes are in flux in Germany at the present time.

The Ticklish Business of Sie and Du

All members of a family say "Du" to each other. Children are always addressed with "Du", even by teachers and strangers, until mid-adolescence.

Colleagues in the professions and office workers mostly say "Sie", while blue-collar workers and military comrades say "Du" to each other.

In German social life, "Du" and first name usage among adults connotes a very close, intimate friendship. — Young people are quicker at making "Du" friends.

"Du" and "Sie" — More Than Just a Different Custom

"Typical German formality", Americans may think when they hear how some Germans say *Sie* and *Herr* to each other even after several years of acquaintance.

It is true that *Du* (used with the first name) is the general intimate form and *Sie* (used with the family name) the more formal one. But to a German *Frau* or *Herr* and *Sie* simply does not sound as formal as Mrs., Miss or Mr. sounds to an American. On the other hand, calling a German by his first name and *Du* can imply greater intimacy than using first names in America.

It Depends. . .

What to call someone depends very much on the social environment. For instance, colleagues in an office may call each other by the family name and *Sie* for years, and yet the atmosphere can be very cordial and informal. Generally, *Sie* is used among white-collar employees, professional people and civil servants, while manual workers, lower echelon and very young employees almost always will say *Du* to each other (but *Sie* to the boss; as a rule the

boss will also use *Sie* and the family name in talking to his workers). In small communities, most people will say *Du* to each other. Military comrades use *Du* (but in dealings between officers and servicemen, the *Sie* form will be used). Also members of the Social Democratic Party, the Green Party, and trade unionists normally use *Du*. The *Du* in all these cases expresses feelings of solidarity.

Men Are Quicker at "Du"

A survey revealed that about one quarter of all adult Germans quickly change to *Du* after having made friends, but more than 40 per cent wait for quite some time. Men use *Du* twice as often with friends as women do. *Du* is always used within the family and with children up to mid-adolescence, and, of course, among lovers. Most young people, up to their mid-twenties, normally use the *Du* among each other.

Thus, university students will say *Du* to each other, but *Sie* to their teachers and professors and vice versa, unless the professors are exceptionally progressive-minded and insist on *Du*.

Always Use "Sie" First

The foreigner is always well advised to use *Sie* (and the family name) first and then to play it by ear. Usually it is the older person who suggests the switch to *Du* ("Sagen wir doch du zueinander" or "Duzen wir uns doch!").

If two Germans decide to associate on a *Du* basis, they may even celebrate the occasion by way of *Brüderschaft trinken* (drink to brotherhood): wine or beer glass in hand, the two people hook arms and each sips from his own glass. Then they shake hands, and kiss lightly if women, and announce their first name, such as "ich heiße Monika".

Like many other old customs, however, this *Brüderschaft* ceremony is regarded as somewhat ridiculous by the younger generation.

Du Related to Thou

When looking at the historical development of languages, it is interesting that the Germans kept the informal *Du* at all. In the English language, the "you" once was the formal mode of address which centuries

Du and Sie
(continued)

ago won out over the informal "thou", a form directly related to the German *Du*.

Actually, the whole *Sie* and *Du* business touches upon a significant difference that exists in the attitudes and conventions of Germans and Americans and that results from quite different social traditions.

While Americans, in becoming acquainted, automatically try to create a relaxed, informal atmosphere, Germans (and most other Europeans, too, for that matter) react with a kind of polite formality.

Germans accept the distance between strangers as a normal fact of life, and the *Sie* means just that. No offense meant!

The Man Should Walk on the Left Side

Many young people in Germany will tell you that it does not matter who should walk on the left: the man or the woman. Many of the older ones, however — or perhaps the girl you wish to impress with your good manners! — will note it immediately if the foreign visitor makes an effort to adapt to German custom.

As a basic rule, a man walks on the left side of a woman in Germany — in the streets and everywhere. The place on the right is always the "place of honor", so to speak.

When two men and one woman are walking together, the woman should walk in the middle. If a man walks with two women, he would normally stay in the middle, so as to devote equal attention to both.

Keep to the Side of the Traffic

Considerate men do not always follow this rule. When walking down a very narrow street or wherever traffic is so heavy that it might disturb or even endanger the woman at his side, the man keeps to the side where the traffic is.

Why this rule of keeping to the left? Two explanations have been heard for this custom. One explanation sounds very romantic. It says that the escort always wanted to be close to the side where the lady's heart was. The second explanation gives a more practical reason, although it is somewhat romantic, too, because it goes back to the times of the medieval knights. Since a knight used to have his sword on his left, it was natural for the woman to go on the other side, where the sword could not disturb her.

Why Walk on the Left?

Normally the escort keeps to the left side.   *"Left is where the heart is."*   *The "sword theory".*

Guten Morgen, Herr Professor! — A Few Words About German Titles

Although titles are certainly no longer as important in Germany as they used to be, it is still true that a person's social prestige is determined by his professional standing and title, more so than in other Western countries.

There are, of course, variations.

In a big city, a title is not taken as seriously as in a small village. Also, younger people are much less impressed by titles than the older generation. The Northern Germans tend to use fewer titles than the Southern Germans. The stranger who wants to get along with the people is well advised if he tries to adapt to the established local usage, although it may seem a little ridiculous at times.

Herr General, Frau Doktor

All German forms of address, with only a very few exceptions, begin with *Herr* or *Frau,* followed by either the title and/or the family name. The holders of any German doctor's degree — not just medical doctors — are addressed as *Herr Doktor So-and-So.* The family name is often left out when addressing doctors of medicine. A university professor is called *Herr Professor,* with or without the family name. (Some younger doctors, however, do not use their titles).

In speaking to a person holding several titles, only the higher one is used. In addressing a letter to a German professor, you would write *Herrn Professor Dr. Meier,* but the salutation would be: *Sehr geehrter Herr Professor!* or *Sehr geehrter Herr Professor Meier!*

The mayor of a town is called *Herr Bürgermeister.* Judges are addressed as *Herr Richter.* Common names for clergy are *Herr Pfarrer* or *Herr Pastor,* and for Catholic clergy *Hochwürden.*

A *Minister* is not a clergyman in Germany, but a government department head. With government officials, the rank or title is preceded by *Herr* (or *Frau*): *Herr Minister, Frau Staatssekretär, Herr Ministerpräsident, Herr Botschafter,* etc. The three highest-ranking personalities in the federal German government are addressed as *Herr Bundespräsident* (foreigners say *Eure Exzellenz*), *Frau Bundestagspräsidentin* and *Herr Bundeskanzler.*

Members of Parliament are officially called *Herr Abgeordneter,* otherwise simply *Herr So-and-So.*

In the military, the *Herr* is added to the rank: *Herr General, Herr Oberstleutnant, Herr Major, Herr Hauptmann;* also the lowest grades below the non-commissioned officer *(Herr Unteroffizier)* are addressed this way: *Herr Gefreiter.*

Herr Kollege

It is not customary to introduce oneself with one's title or rank, but with the family name only. Also, persons of equal rank do not use their titles when talking with one another. Two professors or two doctors will say *Herr So-and-So* to each other, or *Herr Kollege,* if they belong to the same profession.

Women have it relatively easy in German protocol. They need not address men with their professional titles when meeting them socially, unless the difference in social standing or age is very great. Whether they should use the titles in professional life depends very much on the given circumstances.

A woman with an academic degree is addressed as *Frau Doktor So-and-So* or *Frau Professor.* It is no longer correct — although you may hear it sometimes — to address a married woman with her husband's title (such as *Frau Direktor* or *Frau Präsident*). *Gnädige Frau* (Gracious Lady), which is roughly equivalent to the English "Madam", is always correct when dealing with women of higher status, but it is very formal. Women will only use this form of address when the difference in status is very great.

Nobility

It is impossible in this short space to explain all the intricate ranks of German nobility. One should perhaps note that today, the prefix *von* as well as designations such as *Freiherr* and *Graf* are only considered as part of the family name. The correct form of address is generally *Herr* (or *Frau*) *von So-and-So*, while counts are called *Graf* (or *Gräfin*) *So-and-So*, not *Herr Graf.*

All this may sound complicated, but actually it is not that bad. After all, one does not meet a count or a chancellor every day, and a foreigner will readily be excused if he makes a mistake.

"I'm afraid I am a little prudish, Herr Doktor!"

Meeting, Visiting and Living with Germans

Americans have often asked us why Germans, particularly of the middle and older generations, are so "formal" when meeting people and inviting friends. Customs do differ in this respect, and the reason is to be found in the different historical background.

They Stayed Where They Were

While America is a nation of immigrants, Germany is not. In order to survive in the foreign surroundings, immigrants to the U. S. had to develop forms of behavior that allowed them to quickly get acquainted with all kinds of strangers from vastly different ethnic and cultural backgrounds.

The Germans and all other Europeans have never gone through this experience of amalgamation. They more or less stayed where they were — in a given region, with a given set of traditions and manners that allowed them to get along with a relatively close circle of neighbors, co-workers, and friends. As a result, German language and customs did not develop the same forms that helped Americans to overcome the distance between strangers so easily and quickly.

Even today, Germans don't move about as much as Americans do, and many would rather put up with a long commuting distance or learn another trade than change their place of residence. While in America about one fifth of the population moves every year, the majority of Germans still spend their whole life in the same place or at least in the same region where they were born and grew up, within a circle of people they have known for a long time.

This may be responsible for certain provincial attitudes not only in the more rural areas but also in parts of the larger cities of Germany. For instance, some people may openly stare at you simply because you are a stranger on their street — take it with humor!

Distance Not Seen as Disturbing

When meeting a stranger or a foreigner, the average German will be friendly but will not make a special effort to overcome the distance and the feeling of strangeness. Don't mistake this behavior as coldness or lack of good will; the distance is seen by him or her as the most natural thing in the world, not as a barrier that must be overcome as quickly as possible.

Being situated in the center of Europe, Germany has often had foreign visitors —

from missionaries to occupation troops, merchants, migrant workers, and tourists.

They are nothing uncommon, and few people are likely to approach a person simply because he or she is from another country. On the contrary: upon meeting some Germans (certain landlords, for instance) you may discover open refusal and distrust of all *Ausländer* (foreigners). Don't generalize such experiences, but remember:

You Must Take the Initiative

If you wish to establish social contacts with Germans, the initiative usually must come from your side. Feel your way and be prepared to wait for a personal friendship to develop. Don't be put off by the fact that your neighbor may not have acknowledged your greeting, when you smile or nod the first time. Try it again after you have seen him or her a few times, and you may get quite a different response. The best way to make contacts is probably to join a German-American Club or a German hobby club — sports club, stamp collectors club, or whatever your interests may be.

To emphasize — because it's important if you want to understand the German way of life: Most Germans live in a rather narrow, close network of social relationships which are determined by tradition and custom as well as by the individual's education and job status.

Significance of the Home

Home life is of the greatest significance, both as a shelter from the turmoil and stress of the outside world and as an expression of one's own private standing.

Most German housewives take a great pride in the way their home is equipped and kept up — sometimes even at the cost of cultivating social contacts.

This means that not only for foreigners, but also for Germans who have to move to another location, it may be quite difficult to make new friends.

Being Invited

If you have been formally invited to a private German home you may consider it as a special gesture of friendship. You may expect that your visit has been carefully prepared for: the house will be spick and span, *Kuchen* may have been baked for coffee or a good dinner may have been cooked, and the hosts will be dressed for the occasion (in general, Europeans tend to place more importance on appearance than Americans).

If you are invited for coffee or a meal, be on time and take along a little bouquet of flowers for the hostess. Remove the wrapping before presenting the flowers. (Be careful with red roses — they can be poison ivy if given to the wrong person at the wrong time, because they are usually offered by a lover to his sweetheart. White chrysanthemums are often regarded as burial flowers).

Flowers, Thank-you Note

At a large party with many guests, often flowers are not brought along but sent before the party or on the next day, with a short note. A thank-you note is not expected if you have brought or sent flowers. After a nice party, the wife of the invited couple may call the hostess and say a few words of thanks.

When Invited, Bring Some Flowers

Casual visits are rare, private invitations are a special gesture of friendship. Bring along some flowers for the hostess.

It is customary to take off the wrapping of the flowers before presenting them. Cellophane wrapping is not removed, however.

Red roses may mean "I love you".

Try To Be on Time

Try to be on time — coming much too late makes a bad impression in Germany.

"Entschuldigen Sie bitte, daß ich so spät komme, aber . . ." (up to your imagination!)

Most Germans consider punctuality a great virtue, especially in private appointments. If you have been invited for dinner, you are normally expected to arrive on time. Do not come early, but not later than ten or 15 minutes (naturally, this does not apply to receptions). The long cocktail hour before dinner is not the rule in Germany.

What do you say if you are late anway?

Say: "*Entschuldigen Sie bitte, dass ich so spät komme*" or "*dass ich mich verspätet habe*" or "*dass ich Sie warten liess, aber . . .*" (please excuse me for coming so late, or: for being late, or: for letting you wait, but . . .)

Some standard excuses:

— *Ich hatte noch zu tun*
(I had to finish urgent work)

— *Ich sass im Stau*
(I was caught in a traffic jam)

— *Ich fand keinen Parkplatz*
(I could not find a parking space)

Cream and Sugar? — Ja, bitte!

"Nehmen Sie Sahne und Zucker zum Kaffee?" (Do you take cream and sugar with your coffee?) the hostess asks. The guest either accepts ("Ja, bitte") or says "Nur Sahne bitte" (only cream, please) or explains that he prefers his coffee black: "Nein, danke, ich trinke ihn (den Kaffee) schwarz."

Asking someone to hand you the sugar, you may say: "Würden Sie mir bitte den Zucker reichen?" In handing it over, the other person will say: "Bitte sehr!" and you thank him or her with "Danke sehr!" or "Danke schön!" — "Please help yourself" would be "Bitte, bedienen Sie sich!" in German.

"Bitte, möchten Sie (nehmen Sie) noch ein Stück Kuchen?" (Would you like to have — will you take — another piece of cake?) More formal would be: "Darf ich Ihnen noch ein Stück Kuchen geben?" (May I give you . . .) — "Ja, bitte!" or "Nein, danke!" "Danke" or "Ich danke" alone may also mean "No, thank you."

Eating and Drinking Manners

Germans eat differently from Americans. They keep the fork in the left hand throughout the meal, and the knife in the right. So forks and knives are not changed even after cutting meat. If the left hand is not needed, it is placed on the table beside the plate, not in the lap.

At a German dinner party, the host drinks first, raising his glass to the health of his guests: "Zum Wohl!" "Prost" is rather informal, comparable to "cheers".

Knife and Fork

One of the things that startles most Americans upon their arrival to Germany is the way the Germans eat. Whenever they eat something that requires cutting, they hold the fork in the left hand and the knife in the right, keeping them this way throughout the meal. The knife is also used to push the food onto the fork. If a knife is not needed, the left hand is placed on the table beside the plate, not in the lap.

Most Germans do not cut potatoes with a knife, but use the fork instead. This is a relic from the times when blades were not yet made of stainless steel. Cooked fish is not cut with a knife, but with either a special fish knife or a fork.

The host or the waiter will know that you are finished eating when you place your fork and knife parallel to each other and somewhat diagonally on the plate.

Seldom will you see a German drink plain tap water with his meals — it's either beer or wine, mineral water, or nothing at all.

(continued on page 26)

Eating and Drinking Manners
(continued)

The Host Is the First To Drink

In Germany nobody drinks at a dinner party before the host has drunk. The host first tests the wine for temperature and then fills (or has filled) the glasses of his guests, his own last. He is the first to drink, raising his glass to the woman on his right and toasting to the health of the group. People may then drink as they see fit. The most accepted toast is *Zum Wohl!* (to your health). The host will usually add some words of greeting and good wishes. *Prost* comes closest to "cheers".

Toasting Among the Guests

Toasting among the guests is an old-established German custom, and can even be done from a certain distance, provided one catches the eye of the person one intends to honor. The toaster, with his glass raised, nods towards the person he wants to toast, and she or he will smile back. Then both sip their wine, raise their glasses once more and put them back on the table. The person of higher rank initiates the toast towards his inferior, who is expected to return the toast a little later; between a man and a woman, it is always the man who makes the overture.

Clinking Glasses

As a rule, Germans clink their glasses only when wishing each other luck, or when celebrating some special event such as a birthday or wedding. Only glasses with wine or champagne are clinked together, beer sometimes (at informal occasions), brandy never.

Seating the Guest of Honor

In Germany, a guest of honor is seated to the left of the hostess, if it's a man, and to the right of the host, if it's a woman.

Flowers and Plants in the Windows

Most German housewives take great pride in the looks of their windows. You see fancifully tucked-up curtains everywhere and flowers and potted plants in the windows of most every German house. Contrary to the United States, fly screening is rarely seen here, but there are more curtains and sheers behind the windows.

My Home Is My Castle — Die Wohnung

It must be the cool climate and the long, dark winters that make a cozy home so all-important for the Germans. *Die Wohnung* (dwelling, living place) ranks highest above all other goods, even above the car and vacation trips. Opinion pollsters have indicated that only their health, family and job are closer to the Germans' heart.

Nine out of ten Germans would like to live in their own apartment or house, but only every third family has reached that goal; two thirds live in rented apartments.

Privacy is more important here, in densely populated Central Europe, than in many places in the U. S.

When moving into a new community, Germans usually do not make special efforts to meet their new neighbors. They may make a short visit to the people living next door, but this is not automatically expected of them. It is also not customary that the old-timers come to welcome the newcomers. Getting to know one's neighbors is more or less left to chance.

Germans also tend to close their doors more than Americans do. In addition to the cherished privacy, there is a practical reason for this: heating.

A Tradition of Saving Energy

Although roughly four fifths of all German homes now have central heating, attitudes towards energy saving have not changed substantially from the past when rooms were heated individually. Saving energy is nothing new for German home owners because oil, gas, electricity and coal have always been considerably more expensive in Germany than in America. Most people turn up the heat just in the living room, leaving the rest of the house cooler (each room has its own radiator).

In the summer time, there is no heating, except during cold spells.

Air conditioning is found only in very modern offices, hotels and restaurants.

Daylight is used whenever possible — and it is rarely so hot that one has to close curtains and shutters against too much sunshine.

Many German buildings have entrance hallway lights that are controlled by a timed switch: When you turn the light on, it will go out automatically after a couple of minutes. In many German homes, a small electric appliance *(Durchlauferhitzer)* activates and heats water only when a hot-water faucet is turned on. You will find many gadgets and customs that explain why the average German citizen uses approximately half as much energy as an American.

House Guests

If you have been invited to stay with a German family as a house guest, your hosts may expect you to bring a little *Mitbringsel* (gift) along, perhaps something typical of the U. S. If you do not know your hosts very well, this may present a problem as it is sometimes difficult to judge their interests and tastes from afar. They may just hate maple syrup or the things you get in the usual gift shop! But you can hardly go wrong with a book of photos from your home region, cassettes or records with American folk music, or T-shirts for the kids.

Cherished Privacy

Germans tend to close their office doors rather than leave them open. This is also true for many private homes. Before entering, knock at the door, even if it's "public". "Herein" means "come in".

Germans build more fences than Americans. There are exceptions in modern housing settlements, but usually every house has a fenced-in front yard, and if there is a back yard, this will be fenced-off, too.

When moving to a new neighborhood, do not feel insulted if your neighbors seem to ignore you at first. Getting to know one's neighbors is more or less left to chance.

Living in a German House

Foreign customs can be interesting — even fascinating, but when it comes to living in close contact with the inhabitants of another country, where the different customs really clash, ill feelings often arise from minor misunderstandings.

Even simple practical differences can present considerable problems. For instance, German laws and customs with regard to apartment leasing differ considerably from those in the United States.

Renting an Apartment

First of all, *finding* a suitable apartment at a reasonable price is not at all easy. Luxury apartments at high rents are offered everywhere, but normal, nice, comfortable and reasonably priced apartments or houses can be difficult to find — particularly in the urban centers of Southern Germany.

House hunting will take considerable time, patience, and effort, unless you have a lot of money to spend.

The size of homes is determined by the number of rooms: If you want three bedrooms, living room, and dining room —

look for a *5 Zimmer* home. Bathroom, toilet, kitchen and hall areas are not included in the room count. *2½ Zimmer* does not mean bedroom, living room plus shower/bath (American style), but two rooms plus a small sized room.

Furnished apartments are relatively rare in Germany. Unfurnished usually means that — no light fixtures, no built-ins, no closets, no kitchen cupboards or appliances — just bare walls.

Unless you are lucky and find a place through friends or through a newspaper ad (best days for rentals are Wednesdays and Saturdays), you will probably need the services of a rental agent or real estate broker (*Wohnungs-* or *Hausmakler, Immobilienmakler*).

In dealing with a *Makler*, keep in mind that normally you don't pay any kind of administrative fees (*Bearbeitungsgebühren*) and you should not pay the commission (*Courtage*) before actually signing the rental agreement (*Mietvertrag*). The normal fee for the agent is between one and three months rent.

You may be asked to pay *Mietvorauszahlung* (advance payments on the rent) or a contribution to renovating costs or for taking over built-ins.

If *Kaution* is demanded by the landlord, this means he wants to have "security" in case of damage to his property. This sum, equal to one or three months' rent and payable in addition to your first month's rent, will be refundable in whole or in part, according to the rental contract. It has to be securely deposited with a bank or *Sparkasse,* and the account should be in your and the landlord's name, so that you will also receive interest payments.

Be sure to make note of the condition of the property — especially all damages or defects that already exist — before moving in (and get it witnessed by the landlord!).

Extra Costs and Duties

The tenant is responsible for the regular maintenance of the rooms, especially interior painting and decorating.

Utility services — electricity, gas, water,

Living in a German House

(continued)

The wrong plug?

heating, garbage pick-up, etc. — usually cost extra — as may garage rent, use of the garden, chimney sweep, janitor service, etc. In some places, the tenant (mostly the groundfloor tenant) may be responsible for sweeping the sidewalk and clearing away the snow.

Ask questions about all of the above points before you sign, also about the notice of termination (*Kündigung*), which is often longer here than in the U. S. Try and get someone experienced to go through the papers with you.

General Rules

As a general rule, no noisy activities are allowed in German apartment houses before 7 or 8 AM, between 1 and 3 PM and after 10 PM. There are restrictions on the times for lawn mowing, etc. Sunday is generally considered a day of rest.

Problems with Electrical Appliances

Electricity in Germany is 220 Volt — 50 cycle (in USA 110 Volt — 60 cycle).

For appliances brought from the U. S. you need a voltage transformer (*Transformator*). You must be sure, however, to use the right size lest you either burn out the transformer (with danger of fire) or ruin the appliances. Each appliance has a listed wattage and the transformer used must have at least the capacity of that wattage (1 kilowatt = 1,000 watts). On some appliances, you will find amperage instead of wattage listed. In this case, multiply the amperage by the voltage to obtain the wattage.

Lamps can be converted by changing the plug and using German light bulbs. German lampshades will not fit American or English lamps.

Not suitable for use are American TV sets, record players, tape recorders, and electric clocks because of the difference in cycles.

Many German homes still do not have a central hot water system, therefore German washers and dishwashers have built-in water heaters. An American washer or dryer may work with a transformer built in it, but you should have it checked out first by an experienced electrician.

German washing machines usually have a choice of four temperatures : 30° C (cool), 40° C (warm), 60° C (hot), 95° C (very hot).

Nearly all German wall sockets are of the round prong type, and only the *Schuko* plug, fitted with a special grounding wire, will fit into it. Electrical shops should have adapter plugs (*Zwischenstecker*) to convert flat prongs to round.

Other Household Problems

Curtains and draperies are expensive. The curtain rod system is different, too, so if you bring curtains, bring the rods, hooks and installation devices.

Bed linen here is quite different from what you're used to. Germans start with a bottom sheet (*Bettuch*) on the mattress, but instead of adding further layers (top sheet and blankets), they use a comforter — or a blanket — enclosed in removable sheeting (*Bettbezug*).

Sperrmüll

If you wonder about the piles of bulky trash items that decorate the streets of your area every few months, often thoroughly searched by bargain hunters before being hauled away by the garbage men —

this is *Sperrmüll*. The day on which you can get rid of all the large junk that won't fit in your garbage can (except for construction materials, auto parts, and old tires) is known as *Sperrmülltag*. Ask your landlord or the neighbors for the dates and times, and then put everything out on the curb the night before.

On certain days of the month, the Red Cross and other welfare organizations collect bundled newspapers and magazines as well as old clothes that have been placed on the curb of the street.

In most German towns there are also containers for recycling paper, glass, plastic, clothing and batteries.

When Moving Out

And one final tip when you move out: do terminate any insurance contracts in time, and in writing, as otherwise they will continue even if you don't pay anymore and you will be obliged to pay further. The same is true of newspaper subscriptions and similar regular services — always terminate them in writing.

Getting a Phone

When renting a house or apartment, find out if there is a telephone already installed which you can take over from the previous tenant. This will cost you less time and money than getting a completely new installation. The post office will give you a form called *Antrag auf Übertragung eines Fernsprechanschlusses*. You fill out the form and send it to the respective *Anmeldestelle für Fernmeldeeinrichtungen*. (In Germany, all telecommunications are operated by the post office). The form for applying for a new installation is called *Antrag auf Einrichtung eines Fernsprechanschlusses*.

Once your telephone is installed and connected, you become a subscriber and are obliged to pay your monthly phone bill (*Fernmelderechnung*). It may be higher than you expect, as telephoning is considerably more expensive in Germany than in the U.S., particularly long-distance. More about using the phone in Germany on pages 81 — 86.

If You Want To Live Here: The Red Tape

Private Americans and other non-EC citizens who intend to live in the Federal Republic of Germany have to go through a lot of red tape before settling down, especially if they are planning to work here.

Registration

First, anyone setting up a new residence in Germany (no matter whether he or she is a German citizen or a foreigner) is required by German law to register (*anmelden*) immediately — within three to seven days — with the local registration office (*Einwohnermeldeamt* or *Polizeirevier*). A form called *Anmeldung* (you can get it in stationery shops or the registration office itself) must be filled out, and an adult member of the family or an authorized agent (with a written power of attorney) must submit the form together with the passports of all members of the family.

Don't forget to "de-register" with the local authorities before you leave. Go to your local registration office and fill in a green *Abmeldung* form. Be sure to take your passport and your *Anmeldung* form with you. If you are receiving *Kindergeld*, be sure also to inform the *Kindergeldkasse* at the *Arbeitsamt* that you will be leaving.

For any stay exceeding three months, foreigners aged 16 and older need a German residence permit (*Aufenthaltserlaubnis*).

Residence Permit, Work Permit

You will need a work permit (*Arbeitserlaubnis*) if you wish to take up paid employment. The permit is limited to your specific job. The residence permit and the work permit should be obtained before leaving for Germany. You apply for these permits at the German diplomatic or consular representation in the area where you live. You may also need a certificate of employment from your home employer (if you are staying on that company's payroll while working in Germany), your national or an international driver's license, and documents for car transfer.

If you have not yet obtained a residence permit before leaving your home country, you must — after being registered — submit an application (*Antrag auf Erteilung einer Aufenthaltserlaubnis*) with the local aliens department (*Ausländeramt*, or whatever the respective local authority may be called). Take your passport, two photos, and a copy of your *Einwohnermeldebestätigung*. You may also be required to take a medical examination at the public health department.

First, a temporary permit is granted for three months; thereafter it can be extended for up to one year. If you stay longer, you must renew the permit regularly before it expires.

The work permit is issued by the employment office (*Arbeitsamt*) of the German community where you live. You need a residence permit which does not automatically exclude application for a work permit, your passport, and a form filled out by your future employers stating that they wish to employ you.

In general, work permits are available to non-Germans only if a German or other EEC-citizen cannot fill the job. — A special work permit is issued to foreigners married to Germans.

The work permit, too, must be renewed regularly and in time.

*Street restaurant
in the historic city
center of Nürnberg*

(c) ZEFA-Damm

An abundance of flowers and plants before and behind windows are typical of German homes.

(c) Wolfgang Kunz/Bilderberg

Radio and TV

Americans, being used to commercial TV and radio, often think that in Germany the networks are government-controlled. This is not the case, however. The large radio and TV networks (*ARD* and *ZDF*) are non-profit "public" corporations. They are supervised by advisory boards (*Rundfunkräte*) made up of representatives of the political parties represented in the state parliaments and of the major professional and social groupings such as the trade unions, churches, education, youth organizations, etc.

No commercials interrupt these "public" programs. Advertising is nevertheless an important source of income, but it is packaged into several compact short broadcasts at the beginning of the evening's program (between 6 and 8 p. m. and never on Sundays).

The networks' major source of income is the fee each set owner pays to the G. E. Z. (*Gebühreneinzugszentrale der Rundfunk-*

anstalten) every month. The *Bundespost* gets 23 per cent of this fee in payment for providing the towers, transmitters, cables and other equipment needed to broadcast the programs. The rest of the money goes to the networks.

Upon getting a radio or TV set, you fill in a form (*Rundfunkanmeldung*) which can be obtained at all banks. Conditions and methods of payment are printed on these forms.

Besides the "First" (*ARD*) and "Second" (*ZDF*) national programs, the so-called "Third" program is a regional one, produced and broadcast by the individual *ARD* stations.

For a number of years, commercial radio and TV programs (cable and satellite) have been operating in West Germany, too (SAT 1, 3 SAT, RTL plus, etc.). Which of these will be able in the long run to compete with the established public corporations is an open question.

*The two traditional TV networks, **ARD** and **ZDF**, still dominate the West German media scene, although private and commercial television has been active for several years as well.*

"What, No PTA?" — School Life Is Different

German children spend fewer hours at school than American ones, generally staying only until noon or 1 or 2 PM. In the afternoon, German children must sit down to a heavy load of homework.

Living in a German town you will soon notice that contrary to the US the school does not play any particular role in the social life of the community.

It's a totally different tradition. Almost all schools are public, set up and financed by the state, and the teachers are civil servants, hired and paid by the state school authorities. There are no local school boards and no PTA's (although teachers and parents do meet regularly at *Elternabend*). People are much less directly involved with school matters than in the States. The standard of teaching and exams is relatively equal throughout the country. Curricula, however, differ to a great extent.

Three Main Streams

Kindergartens are separate from the public school system. — In the first four grades of school, all children are educated together in the *Grundschule* (elementary school). Then, mostly with a two-year transition period and depending on their abilities, they may attend either the *Hauptschule* (general junior high school, up to grade 9), *Realschule* (junior high school, up to grade 10), *Gymnasium* (academically oriented junior/senior high school, up to grade 13), or a combination of them all, *Gesamtschule* (comprehensive school).

"All Business"

German schools are "all business," strictly for learning, and not much goes on in the way of social events. They do have regular excursion days (*Wandertag*) and take annual class trips (*Klassenreise*).

Only graduates of a *Gymnasium* (or holders of an equivalent degree) can attend a university, where the emphasis is placed upon specialization in an academic or highly technical field.

Many of the fields taught in American colleges are not to be found at the university but rather at technically-oriented schools of higher education.

Many teenagers learn an occupation in an apprenticeship combined with vocational school.

German students spend less time in school than Americans and tend to separate their private lives more from school matters:

Going to Church?

"Religion: It scarcely plays any role today in the land where the Reformation was born. American religion has simple messages to present to churches that are often packed. German churches are scholarly, liberal — and empty." This is how an American journalist described the situation of the churches in Germany. An overstated judgment, but with a grain of truth in it.

School Life . . .

(continued)

there are hardly any extra-curricular activities, and the American student will look in vain for commencement ceremonies, school rings, yearbooks, honor societies, or university football clubs.

The traditional fraternities still do exist, although they play a role only in the old South-German university towns. Elsewhere, the only visible student associations are the political ones, but their importance has diminished considerably in the last 20 years.

Two Big Churches

The majority of the West German population belong to either the Roman Catholic or the Evangelical-Lutheran Church (about half and half), but most of them do not participate actively in church affairs.

Only some 25 per cent of Catholics go to church regularly, and only 5 per cent of Protestants.

On the whole, relations between churches and their members are much less close and personalized here than in the States. Except perhaps for small Catholic congregations, it means little for a person's social standing whether he is an active church-goer or not.

Through treaties with the German government, the big churches have a guaranteed annual income from their members: if a taxpayer lists his religious affiliation, a church tax is collected by the revenue office and given to the church of his choice.

As a result of historical developments, Northern Germany is primarily Protestant, while the South and West of the country are primarily Catholic. The pattern has changed somewhat, however, on account of post World War II refugee migrations and the population's increasing mobility.

Your Account With a German Bank

West Germany is "overbanked" — there are about 4,800 banks, including some 600 savings banks (*Sparkassen*), with a total of 44,700 offices — one for every 1,400 inhabitants. The post office, too, offers extensive banking services everywhere.

To open an account is easy; you merely have to offer identification. There are checking and transfer accounts (*Girokonto*) and savings accounts (*Sparkonto*).

If your initial deposit is an American check, it may take up to three weeks to be credited to your account. Cashing foreign-currency checks or remitting foreign currency is expensive.

Pay Your Bills by "Überweisung"

Perhaps the most surprising feature to an American is the use of so-called "transfer orders" (*Überweisungen*), by which you direct your bank to transfer a particular sum from your *Giro* account to the account of someone else, even if it is with another bank in another city; this will be accomplished within a few days. In other words,

you do not need to write checks and mail them individually to your suppliers, but rather prepare transfer orders on your bank's specially-provided forms and deliver them or mail them to your bank. They will deduct the sum from your account and, through the banks' clearing system, eventually the credit will appear on your supplier's bank statement with a copy of the transfer order you wrote.

Automatic Services

Standing orders (*Dauerauftrag*) and automatic collections from your account for regular but varying payments (*Abbuchung*) are also very common services of German banks.

Bank statements (*Kontoauszüge*) will be sent to you (at cost) or you can pick them up at the bank.

Checks (*Schecks*) are also available. If you mail a check to someone else in Germany, be sure to mark it with two lines across the left upper corner, adding the words *nur zur Verrechnung* (for deposit only). The safest way to mail a check is by *Brief mit Wertangabe*. The check will not be returned to you

after cashing but your bank statement will show you when the amount has been deducted.

The Eurocheque

A special feature are the "eurocheques" which you can ask for after having properly conducted your checking account for several months. Your "eurocheque" is guaranteed by your bank for up to DM 400,— in most European countries, so you can use it to obtain cash from banks as well as to pay bills in shops, hotels, and restaurants. When writing out an eurocheque, you are expected to write your eurocheque *Kartennummer* (number of the EC card) on the reverse side of the cheque, and to present your eurocheque card when handing over the cheque.

In German Restaurants and Hotels

Eating Out

The time will come in Germany when you just have to find a place to eat without the help of a German friend or a restaurant guide.

"Fast food" is not quite as available in Germany as it is in the States, although chances are that in or near any railway station you will hit upon a *Schnellimbiss* (snack bar) or a *Pizzeria*.

But perhaps you would prefer going to a German restaurant offering a full range of meals. How do you avoid the fancy places with astronomical prices? Just look for the menu posted at the street front — it will show you the price range and choice of food available.

From Ratskeller to Snack Bar

The variety of eating and drinking places in Germany is enormous. In the smaller towns the best places to eat are usually the hotels. A *Gasthof, Gasthaus, Gaststube* and *Gastwirtschaft* is (or includes) a restaurant where you can have a regular sit-down meal.

The fare offered in the more pretentious German restaurants has changed a lot in the last decades. With growing prosperity and availability of first-class ingredients, a rather sophisticated gourmet cuisine has come into being. Some top German restaurants come close to the best in French cooking now, and of course their prices are top-notch to match.

A *Weinstube* (wine parlor) usually does not serve complete lunches and dinners, but it can provide you with substantial snacks with your wine.

A *Bräu* (restaurant often featuring a special brand of beer), *Bierhalle* and *Bierkeller* (beer cellar) usually has plenty of hearty food on hand as well as beer.

A *Biergarten* (beer garden), to be found mostly in Bavaria, is an open-air beer inn. Usually it offers long tables without tablecloths under shady trees, benches without a backrest, large mugs of beer at reasonable prices and a friendly atmosphere.

A *Café* (not to be mistaken for an American coffee-house) sometimes offers hot dishes, too. At any rate, it can produce enough incidental food to satisfy any reasonable person. A *Konditorei* is a pastry shop (see also page 56).

(continued on page 41)

Meal Times

In many German restaurants, hot food (*warme Speisen*) is to be had only during the lunch and dinner hours (snack bars, of course, are an exception). You may be able to get hot food in the afternoon or late at night, but don't count on it.

Mahlzeit!

Sometimes you hear Germans greet each other with *"Mahlzeit"* at lunchtime (and often throughout the afternoon). *"Gesegnete Mahlzeit"* means literally "may your meal be blessed" but the more general meaning is "I hope you will enjoy (or have enjoyed) your meal".

A *Ratskeller* is the basement of the city hall (*Rathaus*). The city fathers once retired to a *Ratskeller* table to tip a few and take a meal. Many a *Ratskeller* has disappeared.

Wherever a small-town *Ratskeller* survives, the beer and filet steaks are likely to be better than anywhere else in town.

In most German towns, there are now a large variety of foreign restaurants — Chinese, Greek, Italian places, steak houses, pizzerias, and what have you.

A *Selbstbedienungs-Restaurant* is similar to the American self-service cafeteria.

Lokal and *Kneipe* are colloquial words for pubs or bars.

Fast Food — Snack Bars

A *Schnellimbiss*, *Schnellgaststätte* or *Imbißstube* is a snack bar. At a *Schnellimbiss* you will be able, for instance, to get a couple of sausages with bread and mustard (*Würstchen mit Brot und Senf*) and a soft drink or beer for a reasonable price. You usually eat standing at a counter or a small round table.

The *Bratwurst* is fat, white and spicy, the *Currywurst* is similar but served with a curry catsup; *Bockwurst* is longer and red, something like a thicker American hot dog. The *Frankfurter* is thinner and usually sold in pairs. — At an *Imbiss* sausages are eaten using the fingers, often with the help of a small cardboard slip. You don't get a bun, though often a slice of bread or a small roll is served with your sausage.

Sandwiches are usually open-face, with no bread on top (an exception are those on a roll). Most common are *Schinkenbrot* (ham on bread) and *Käsebrot* (cheese on bread).

Other fast-food places sell pizza and US-style hamburgers and hot dogs as well as the universal grilled chicken (*Brathähnchen*). You also find a growing number of crepes and croques stands in Germany today.

In big cities, some department stores have installed "chic fast food" counters, where luxury items like oysters, champagne, etc. are offered to busy shoppers. Even some smaller shops (butchers, bakers, etc.) are providing quick snacks now.

Restaurant Manners

Many Americans wonder whatever happened to "ladies first" when they see that German men often precede women in entering a restaurant. This exception from the rule is clearly a remainder from times when the man was the one to decide whether the locality was fit for the woman to enter. In entering first, he could also screen her from curious stares and relieve her of the task of choosing a table.

As a rule today, the man opens the restaurant door so that the woman can enter first. She then steps aside and lets him guide the way in.

No Hostess to Greet and Seat You

Contrary to American custom, there are no hostesses in German restaurants to greet and seat you. Normally, you look for a free table yourself. Only in restaurants of the higher price range will a waiter approach you and suggest a table or lead you to the table that has been reserved for you. In this case, the woman goes behind the waiter, followed by the man.

(continued on page 42)

Eating Out
(continued)

"Herr Ober!"

The wardrobe is *die Garderobe* in German. The sign "*Für Garderobe kann nicht gehaftet werden*" means that all articles are left at owner's risk.

All Waiters Are "Herr Ober"

Asking for the menu, say "*Würden Sie mir bitte die Karte bringen?*" Never ask for *das Menü* in this case, as that would mean ordering a complete meal! The waiter (*der Kellner*) is addressed as "*Herr Ober*" (no matter whether he is the headwaiter — *Oberkellner* — or not), the waitress as "*Fräulein*". In small towns and villages, the local *Gasthaus* or inn is often a family enterprise, where the proprietor and his wife wait on their guests themselves. In such a place, you would call the proprietor "*Herr Wirt*" and his wife "*Frau Wirtin*".

Ever Ordered Dinner in German?

Ordering a dinner à la carte is difficult for a foreigner, though fortunately most waiters in German restaurants know a little English. It's simplest to order a *Gedeck* or *Menü* which is a complete dinner with soup (*die Suppe*) and dessert (*der Nachtisch*). On the *Tageskarte* of the menu you will find those dishes that change every day. For à la carte-ordering, see our vocabulary on pages 131-132.

Bread or rolls are rarely served with hot meals in the average German restaurant. If you order them, there will be a small charge, and also for butter which must be ordered.

And here is an example of how an ordering conversation could go:

Waiter: *Haben Sie schon gewählt?*

1st Customer: *Ja, ich nehme das Gedeck Nummer I.*

W.: *Und Sie?*

2nd C.: — *Ich möchte die Tagessuppe und die Forelle blau.*

3rd C.: — *Was können Sie denn heute besonders empfehlen?*

W.: *Sehr gut ist der Schweinebraten.*

3rd C.: — *Gut, dann nehme ich den.*

W.: *Und was trinken Sie?*

1st C.: — *Ein Schoppen Weisswein, ein Mineralwasser, und für mich ein Bier.*

W.: *Danke sehr.*

When calling the place, the conversation could go like this:

Gasthaus zur Post! Guten Tag!

Guten Tag! Ich möchte bitte für heute abend einen Tisch reservieren.

Um wieviel Uhr?

Um 20.00 Uhr.

Auf welchen Namen?

Auf den Namen Miller.

Und wieviel Personen?

Für drei Personen.

Also: Eine Reservierung für heute abend, 20.00 Uhr, drei Personen auf den Namen Miller. Richtig?

Ja, richtig. Danke schön. Auf Wiedersehen!

Service is slow in some German restaurants. Not only may you have to wait quite a while for your meal but it often takes a considerable amount of time to get hold of the waiter when you want to pay. If you call him and he replies *"sofort"* (right away), don't take it literally — it may take him another five minutes. At any rate, you will never be pushed out after a meal by over-zealous waiters.

Paying the Check

How does one ask for the check? *"Herr Ober, ich möchte zahlen!"* or *"die Rechnung, bitte!"* or very short, *"Zahlen, bitte!"* Normally, you pay the waiter in cash directly at your table, rarely at the counter or cash register.

(continued on page 44)

Sharing Tables

Except for high-priced restaurants, the practice of sharing tables if there is no free table left is quite common, particularly in southern Germany. Of course, one must ask permission of those seated at the table before seating oneself: *"Entschuldigen Sie, ist hier noch frei?"* The answer is mostly, *"Ja, bitte sehr!"*

Just before starting to eat, those sharing a table often wish each other *"Guten Appetit!"* The answer is *"Danke"*. *"Gleichfalls"* means "the same to you".

Eating Out (continued)

Tipping

10 to 15 per cent for service (*Bedienung*) and 14 per cent for value-added tax (*Mehrwertsteuer*) is included in the price.

Although an extra tip is not necessary, most people do round the bill off to the nearest Mark or more, according to the amount to be paid and the service rendered. For instance, if the check amounts to DM 16,80 you may say *"Achtzehn Mark, bitte!"* to the waiter, thus indicating that you expect change only for eighteen marks and that the rest is for him. The tip is given directly to the waiter upon paying and is not left on the table when leaving the place. But to repeat: you are under no obligation to tip, especially not if the service has been poor.

Checks, Credit Cards

Paying by check or credit card is still not as customary in Germany as it is in the United States, but gradually these methods of payment are becoming more popular over here, too. Presently, about a million (of 60 million) Germans own credit cards, over 16 million eurocheque cards.

Closing Times

How late at night will you be able to get a beer in a German *Gaststätte*?

Closing hours for restaurants are set by the authorities of the federal states.

Berlin has no officially-fixed closing hours at all. Hamburg has none for Friday and Saturday nights, with 4 a.m. being the general limit on normal weekdays. In other states, this limit may be fixed at 1 or 2 a.m. This does not mean, however, that places cannot close earlier — many do.

It is also common to grant waivers in nightlife districts.

Ruhetag means closing day, *Betriebsferien* means closed for vacation (*Urlaub*).

Teen Curfew

American parents should know that in Germany, teenagers under 16 are not allowed to visit bars and discos unless accompanied by a "responsible adult". Teenagers 16 to 18 may visit these places until midnight. To enforce the Youth Protection Law, young people's ID cards are checked regularly by the German police. Parents are held responsible.

"Restrooms"

Europeans often smile when they learn about American efforts to avoid using the word "toilet". Words like powder room, rest room, etc. are not known in Germany.

Germans have always been less prudish and more direct in such matters. In a German restaurant it is absolutely normal, if you want to go to the bathroom, to ask a waiter *"Wo ist die Toilette, bitte?"*

Der Stammtisch

A Table for the Regulars

In many a German *Gasthaus* or *Wirtshaus* (inns and taverns) you will find one special table reserved for the local cronies who regularly come together there, usually toward evening, to have a beer, argue politics and perhaps play skat (a card game) or dice. This table, with its bare wooden top polished from daily use, frequently bears a huge ashtray or just a sign with the inscription *"Stammtisch"* (regular table), often accompanied by a small pennant.

So when looking for a table, don't be surprised if the management suggests you choose a table other than this one. Of course, if you return often enough, you may eventually become a member of the *Stammtisch* yourself . . .

An der Theke

As every real pub-goer knows, the best place in an inn is at the *Theke* (bar), because this is where the beer flows. This is also the place where it is easy to get talking to one's neighbor.

In some regions, glasses of *Theke* drinkers are refilled without special order — until you place a beer mat on the top of your glass, a sign that you have had enough and want to pay.

The Money

"Haben Sie's klein?" (Do you have coins?) — *"Leider nein, ich habe nur einen Fünfzig-Mark-Schein!"* (Sorry no, I only have a 50 Mark bill).

There are nine different coins in Germany, i. e. *ein Pfennig, zwei Pfennig, fünf Pfennig, zehn Pfennig (ein Groschen), fünfzig Pfennig, eine Mark, zwei Mark, fünf Mark* and *zehn Mark*. In banknotes, there are: *fünf Mark, zehn Mark, zwanzig Mark, fünfzig Mark, hundert Mark, fünfhundert Mark,* and *tausend Mark* bills.

Beer and Wine — But No Ice Water!

No ice water on the table

"Ein großes Pils" ("eine Maß" in Bavaria)

Germans, it is true, drink a lot of beer — 180 liters annually per head of the adult population — but they drink even more coffee. Soft drinks follow in the third place, then come milk, mineral waters, tea, fruit juices and wine (21 liters per head).

Perhaps because of the cool climate, the custom of automatically serving ice water in restaurants is not known. Hardly ever will you see a German drink plain water with meals, mostly beer or wine instead. Waiters will look at you strangely and claim it's unhealthy if you order tap water (*Leitungswasser*) — but they will bring it if you insist, probably thinking secretly that you want to down a pill! Of course you may drink mineral water (*Mineralwasser*), fruit, or a soft drink — or nothing at all. Nobody drinks coffee with warm meals in Germany, although sometimes afterwards.

Germans like their beer cool, but not ice-cold. It is served either by the bottle (*Flasche*) or on draft (*vom Faß*). Average places will usually have only a local or nationally known brand; fancier establishments will serve several well-known brands. *Ein Schoppen* means a quarter of a

At a German Hotel

Beer and Wine

(continued)

liter (approximately half a pint) of open wine. $\frac{1}{2}$ Fl. means a half bottle.

When wine is served, the waiter will first show the bottle label to the person who ordered it and will then pour a small amount into his or her glass. The guest samples the wine — with a connoisseur's air — to see if it is all right and neither too cold nor too warm, and then nods his approval.

Before the first sip of beer or wine, raise your glass toward your companion and say *"Zum Wohl"* or *"Prost"* — both mean "To your health".

How to Find a Room

The safest way is to reserve a room in advance, either through a travel agency or, if you know a hotel, by calling or by writing (English will do).

If you arrive without a reservation, in many German towns you can make use of the services of a room referral agency, called *Zimmernachweis,* which often is in or near the railway station. It charges a small fee for locating a room in the price range you indicate. You can also just try the hotels that come along your way.

In addition to hotels, look for signs that say "Pension". *Pensionen* are generally cheaper and plainer than hotels and often have no rooms with bath.

"Fremdenzimmer" or *"Zimmer frei"* means rooms in private homes.

(continued on page 48)

At a German Hotel (continued)

Motels are rare in Germany.

The most reasonable overnight lodgings for young people are the youth hostels *(Jugendherbergen)*. They are clean and generally easily accessible. Each individual who wants to stay in a youth hostel must have a membership card. You would do well to get one before leaving the States, as the charge is fairly high in Germany. A disadvantage is that they all have a strict curfew.

More Single Rooms

In big cities, taking a chance in looking for a hotel room can be risky, as often there are conventions or fairs going on that occupy all available hotel rooms.

There are more single rooms *(Einzelzimmer)* available here than in most U. S. hotels. They are relatively more expensive than two-bed rooms *(Doppelzimmer)* and often smaller than what Americans are used to.

If you wish to have a room with private bath and toilet *(mit Dusche* (shower)/*Bad* (bath) *und W. C.)*, both must be specifically ordered but are not always available in the more moderately priced hotels. If not, there is usually at least one bathroom with shower on each floor at the disposal of all hotel guests *(Etagenbad)*. You should always announce your intention to use the public bath before actually doing so, as a fee will be charged for it.

Room and Board

In resort towns, if you stay at least three days, many places offer inclusive rates for accommodation and meals *(Halbpension* or *Vollpension)*.

Registration Forms

Most Americans traveling in Europe for the first time are a bit irked by the necessity to fill out official forms when registering in a hotel (home address, date of birth, nationality, etc.) These forms must be filled out by all guests, German or foreign. They are required by law, in the interest of public safety.

If you intend to stay in a moderately priced German hotel, bring your soap and wash cloths along. All hotels supply towels, but not all supply soap.

If you find the featherbed cover in your German hotel too warm, ask for a *Wolldecke mit Laken* (blanket and bed sheet).

Continental Breakfast

A "continental breakfast" is usually included in the price of the hotel room. Normally it consists of *Kaffee* or *Tee* (you have a choice), *Brötchen* (white rolls), *Schwarzbrot* or *Vollkornbrot* (brown bread), *Marmelade* (jam) and sometimes *Honig* (honey) and, on request, a soft-boiled egg (*weich gekochtes Ei*) served in a little egg cup. If this is not enough you may order something else, for instance: fried eggs (*Spiegeleier*) or scrambled eggs (*Rühreier*). Germans often eat *Aufschnitt* (assorted cold cuts and cheese) for breakfast. Many German hotels offer breakfast buffets (*Frühstücksbuffet*) which often include a variety of cereals to make your own *Müsli*.

Contrary to American custom, you just get one pot (two or three cups) of coffee or tea for your breakfast, no free refills.

Another difference is that there are relatively few restaurants or cafés that offer breakfast in a German town. For the tourist, breakfast normally is included in the hotel price.

If you go out, it is customary to leave the key (*Schlüssel*) with the reception and ask for it again when coming back (just say your room number, followed by *"Bitte"*).

Paying and Tipping

In all German hotels, pensions etc. you pay when you check out. A service charge will be included in the bill, therefore you are not expected to tip anybody — except for the boy who carried your bag to your room (not under a mark) and the reception clerk, if he has helped you with some special service.

The Portier Helps You

The reception clerk, or in German, the *Portier*, is the man you turn to for almost everything. He speaks English, he will mail your letters, he will take phone calls when you are out. He tells you which train, bus,

"Würden Sie sich bitte eintragen" (Please fill in the registration form) — everybody has to in Germany.

If you stay in a moderately priced hotel, you'd better bring your soap and washcloth with you.

Hotels (continued)

The Old Inns

boat or plane to take. He will get you tickets for them, as well as for theaters, etc. He will recommend the best nightspots, the stores in which to buy souvenirs. He will exchange your money after hours. He will also make reservations for you in the next town as he knows all the *Portiers* there. Even in desperate situations a good *Portier* can almost always find a way — if he is tipped according to the difficulty of the task.

Why is it that so many hotels and inns in German towns have the same names?

In the early Middle Ages lodging for travelers was mostly in the cloisters. The inns and hotels which later sprang up in the neighborhood of these cloisters took names coming from the Old and New Testament. Thus we find hotels called *"Engel"* (Angel), *"Löwe"* (Lion), *"Stier"* (Bull) and *"Adler"* (Eagle) — the symbols of the Evangelists — , *"Drei Mohren"* and *"Drei Könige"* (Three Moors and Three Kings) — the three kings are the symbol of traveling — , *"Rose"* and *"Lilie"* (Rose and Lily) — these flowers represent the Virgin Mary — and the *"Lamm"* (Lamb), the Lamb of God.

Germany's postal system (begun in 1450) also played a role in the naming of the old inns and restaurants. Many of the establishments which sprang up around the postal stations received names such as *"Goldenes Posthorn"*, *"Alte Post"* and *"Neue Post"* or *"Zur Post"*. *"Zum"* or *"Zur"* means "to the sign of".

More About German Food

Most likely you have heard that Germans eat a lot of sauerkraut and prefer heavy meals. There is indeed some truth to that, but it certainly is not the whole truth anymore. While in the past, Germans used to say that *"Der Mensch ißt, um zu leben, lebt aber nicht, um zu essen"* (man eats to live, not lives to eat), over the past thirty years that attitude has changed a lot. In fact, quite the opposite is true today!

Around the turn of the century, the diet of the working class was poor, consisting mainly of potatoes, some vegetables, but little meat. Cookbooks for the upper class, however, reveal that luxury foods were known and enjoyed. These cookbooks include recipes for game, lobster, oysters, as well as exotic fruits and vegetables like avocado, pomegranate, persimmon, broccoli, sweet potatoes, etc.

With the loss of the German colonies following World War I, exotic produce disappeared from the markets and from cookbooks too. During the years of the Third Reich the choice grew even poorer, because Hitler wanted Germany to be independent from other countries and their products.

The Impact of Postwar Prosperity

Immediately after the Second World War, only quantity mattered. Later on when people were no longer hungry, they started to think again about variety and quality of food in their diet. As the German economy prospered, lots of new products appeared in the shops such as frozen food, convenience food, exotic fruits, vegetables, spices, and drinks. Workers from Italy, Greece, Spain, Turkey and other countries brought with them their native foods and opened a variety of ethnic shops and restaurants. Also, as the Germans began to travel more, they discovered new and exciting culinary arts all over the world.

These experiences aroused the curiosity of men and women who were interested in food. How do you prepare the fish soup sampled in Spain? How do you eat an artichoke or an avocado? How do you cook eggplant? While in the past it was considered poor manners to discuss culinary arts and techniques at the table, today such discussions can often be the focus of an evening's conversation. Everyone likes to talk about recipes. Entertaining guests has become a challenge. Germans are proud to offer new dishes. Men exchange addresses of new restaurants like stock tips. No women's magazine can do without new

German Food (continued)

recipes. Specialty magazines concerning food, drink, restaurants, etc. have found a receptive market as have ever growing numbers of cookbooks.

Who Does the Cooking?

That indeed is the question. The German "economic miracle" has taken many women away from their kitchens and into offices and shops. Girls learn a profession but not how to cook. During the week breakfast is a simple meal eaten in a rush. For many, midday meals are served in company cafeterias. Lunch has remained the main meal for many Germans; usually it contains meat or fish, a vegetable, potatoes or noodles, and a dessert. If there isn't a cafeteria, a fast food restaurant is usually not far away. Small snacks are also offered in department stores, at the butcher's, and in delicatessens. There are 22,600 eating establishments in the Federal Republic of Germany which serve quick snacks.

If you look at the shelves in supermarkets, you will see a variety of convenience food items. So what really happens is this: During the week, the family is often fed with as little trouble and loss of time as possible.

Pre-prepared food items such as frozen lasagne save even the most inexperienced cooks from failure.

On weekends, however, meal preparation becomes a time for creative cooking. Cookings skills are no longer cultivated solely by women. Men have discovered the fun of cooking as well. About every fourth German man likes to cook. Sometimes the husband takes over the cooking for the weekend, including the shopping. Men also take part in cooking seminars and spend weekends learning everything about wine, beer or champagne.

Health Foods — A New Trend

Many hotels today serve all sorts of Müsli (whole grain cereals with dried fruit and nuts) for breakfast, showing just how strong the trend for healthier food has become in Germany in the last few years. Not only *Reform-Häuser*, but also *grüne Läden* (alternative health food shops) offer whole grain flours as well as mills to grind your own grains and other naturally grown foods. Home baked bread has become popular again, presenting a challenge to

German bakers who now offer an increasing variety of rolls and bread made from whole grain.

But What Do Germans Really Eat?

The Germans certainly consume a lot of meat, mostly pork, but also quite a lot of beef and poultry, and some lamb and game, adding up to 103 kilos per head per year. Too much meat, the nutritionists say. The consumption of potatoes, once about 186 kilos per head per year, has dropped to about 71 kilos, and today most potatoes are consumed in ready made products such as instant mashed potatoes, potato dumplings, potato pancakes, or French fries. Too much fat, especially butter and cream, is consumed as well. But Germans also eat 77 kilos of vegetables per head per year, which is much more than was eaten 50 years ago.

Where Can You Find Typical German Cuisine?

With all the changes we have mentioned so far, you may well ask if there is still a chance to sample original German cuisine. There is. Each region in Germany still has its own special dishes. You may find them in a *Kneipe* (beer restaurant or pub) or in a *Weinstube*, and sometimes in ordinary middle-class restaurants. First class restaurants may also include regional dishes in their menus. In fact, this is the newest trend in gourmet cooking. The following will give you an idea of which specialties you might find in and around some German towns and regions.

Berlin

Berliner Leber — fried liver with onions, sliced apples, and mashed potatoes.

Aal grün — pieces of poached eel, served in a creamy sauce with herbs, usually dill, and a cucumber salad.

Löffelerbsen — a soup containing dried peas, salt-pork (especially pork ears), and potatoes seasoned with thyme or majoran.

Soleier — pickled eggs, served with salt and mustard. Typical for a *Berliner Kneipe*.

Buletten — fried meatballs, served hot or cold.

Eisbein mit Sauerkraut und Erbsbrei — salted pig knuckles boiled and served with sauerkraut and puree of dried peas, topped with fried onions.

Berliner Pfannkuchen — round yeast cakes filled with plum jam and deep fried in hot fat. These are eaten in many places besides Berlin on New Year's Eve and *Fastnacht*.

Hamburg

Finkenwerder Scholle mit Speck — fried plaice, topped with cubes of fried bacon and served with potato salad.

Büsumer Krabben — small but very tasty shrimps from the North Sea or the Baltic sea. You may select what you want from *Büsumer Krabbensuppe* to *Büsumer Krabbensalat* or *Büsumer Krabbenbrot* (a dark rye bread with scrambled egg and shrimps on top).

Labskaus — a mixture of salted, boiled and minced beef mixed with mashed potatoes and served with a fried egg, matjes herring, pickled red beets and pickled cucumber. It may sound strange to you, but it is indeed a very good dish. Have a *Bier und Köm* (beer and a straight *Schnaps*) with it.

Matjestopf — pickled herring with sliced apples and onion rings in a nice sour cream sauce.

Rote Grütze — summer berries and their juices thickened with cornflour and served with a vanilla-sauce, cream, or simply milk.

Bremen

Grünkohl mit Schlachteplatte und Röstkartoffeln — kale which should be picked after the first frost for then its taste is at its best. *Grünkohl* is seasoned with pork fat and served with *Kasseler* (a special cured pork steak), *Kochwurst*, or *Pinkel* (a very special sausage which you get only in the Bremen region). Very small whole potatoes cooked in their jackets, peeled and fried are a must with this dish.

Heidschnuckenbraten — is a particularly fine lamb roast which is bred in the Lüneburger Heide, east of Bremen.

(continued on page 54)

German Food (continued)

Blaubeerpfannkuchen — pancakes with blueberries added to the dough.

Cologne and the Rhineland

Sauerbraten mit Rosinensauce und Kartoffelklössen — you may already know *Sauerbraten*, but have you tasted the sauce which in the original version is thickened with *Lebkuchen* (Christmas cookies) and has raisins added to it? *Kartoffelklösse* (potato dumplings) and compote of plums or dried fruit go with *Sauerbraten*.

Reibekuchen mit Apfelmus — raw potatoes, onions, salt and pepper made into a dough from which the pancakes are made. You eat them with applesauce or with *Rübenkraut* (syrup from sugarbeets). *Reibekuchen* is sold on the street or in *Bierkneipen*.

Halwe Hahn — A standing offer in every *Kneipe* in Cologne is the *Halwe Hahn* which is a rye roll topped with cheese.

Muscheln — poached mussels served in big bowls together with dark bread. In Düsseldorf's *Altstadt*, many restaurants specialize in a variety of ways to serve mussels. And at very reasonable prices.

Frankfurt and Mainz

Frankfurter Grüne Sauce — a thick sauce prepared with at least seven herbs and served over cooked beef or eggs. Every food shop in Frankfurt sells the herbs for this traditional sauce. Goethe's mother used to prepare this sauce for her famous son.

Mainzer Handkäs mit Musik — this has nothing to do with music. It is a small cheese which is sliced and served with salt, pepper, chopped onions, vinegar and oil. White wine of the region is drunk with it.

Zwiebelkuchen — a flat yeast-cake topped with a thick layer of onions and eggs. It should be served slightly warm and tastes especially good with wine. This is a popular dish in wine growing regions.

Stuttgart

Maultaschen — something like ravioli but bigger and filled with meat or spinach. You can have them in a very hot broth or lavishly covered with brown butter and fried onions.

Spätzle — a type of homemade noodles. The best are made fresh from a simple dough scraped quickly from a wooden board into boiling water. *Spätzle* is eaten with meat and sauce.

Munich

Weißwurst — a white skinned sausage containing pork, veal and selected herbs, served hot with sweet mustard. In Munich one used to say *"die Weißwurst darf das Elf Uhr Läuten nicht hören"*, which means you should eat it before 11 a.m. Nowadays you can get *Weißwurst* any time of the day (with beer of course).

Laugenbrezel — a big brown salty pretzel. Made from a yeast dough it tastes best when really fresh. So if you eat *Weisswurst* in the evening you might not get a fresh *Laugenbrezel* to go with it, and that would be a pity.

Leberkäse — again don't get confused. This is a meatloaf which has nothing whatsoever to do with liver or cheese but is made from minced pork. *Leberkäse* is eaten warm. You may have *Kohlsalat*, a sort of coleslaw, with it and potato salad.

Leberknödel — medium sized dumplings made from minced liver, bread cubes, and lots of parsley. They are served in a hot broth or with sauerkraut and radish salad.

Bayrische Creme — a fluffy and very rich dessert containing eggs, milk, cream, vanilla and gelatin. If you find it on the menu you must try it.

Baden and the Black Forest

If there is one region which can be especially recommended for its excellent cuisine, it is Baden and the Black Forest. Maybe this is because of its nearness to France or because of its mild climate where everything grows well — wine, fruit, vegetables. Even in the small village restaurants, you can expect excellent food.

Badischer Hecht — pike fried with bacon and served with a sour-cream sauce.

Schnecken — snails, served in a soup or with herb butter.

Grünkernsuppe — *Grünkern* is a sort of wheat harvested before it is ripe and then lightly roasted. It has a slightly sweet taste.

Hollerküchle — elderberry blossoms mixed in a dough with wine, flour and eggs and then fried in hot fat and sprinkled with sugar.

Well — this gives you a sample of German food specialties. As you travel around Germany, you will certainly discover even more interesting dishes.

Christmas Time Is Cookie Time

Christmas is the time for traditional cooking. Each German region has its own special Christmas recipes.

Christmas Eve is a very festive evening in which the Christmas tree is lit for the first time and presents exchanged. Among the traditional dishes are:

Heringssalat — a salad with seven ingredients (which means luck for the next year): pickled herring, veal, potatoes, hard boiled eggs, apples, red beets, and pickled gherkins. Originally the days before Christmas were a time of fasting, thus the small amount of meat in this salad marks the end of fasting.

Karpfen blau mit Meerrettichsahne — poached carp with whipped cream seasoned with horseradish.

Sometimes people just eat *Frankfurter Würstchen mit Kartoffelsalat* (small sausages with potato salad), in order to have time to enjoy all the presents and also the cookies.

Der bunte Teller (comparable perhaps to the American Christmas stocking) should contain at least seven different things: *Pfefferkuchen* (small brown cookies with honey and lots of spices — no pepper though); *Nürnberger Lebkuchen* (very rich round cakes made with lots of ground almonds); *Zimtsterne* (whisked white of eggs, ground almonds, sugar and cinnamon, but no flour, are the ingredients of these very fine cookies); *Heidesand* (flat round white cookies, very sweet), brown butter and vanilla are responsible for the fine taste; *Quittenbrot* — thickened and dried puree of quinces, cut into pieces and dusted with sugar; and *Lübecker Marzipan*. Also un-

(continued on page 56)

German Food

An American Discovers German "Kaffee"

(continued)

shelled nuts, oranges or apples, and perhaps a pomegranate are included.

On Christmas day, *Gänsebraten mit Apfelrotkohl* will often be served (roast goose or duck — *Ente* — with red cabbage and apples). While turkey is not the traditional meal, it has become quite popular.

At tea time you ought to find *Dresdner Christstollen* on your plate. This is a very rich yeast loaf with lots of raisins, almonds, and dried sugared fruit. Similar to it, but not as rich, is the *Hamburger Klöben*.

If your hostess has some connection to the eastern part of Germany she may have baked a *Mohnstollen*, which is a yeast-dough covered with a thick layer of crushed poppyseed, almonds, raisins and sugar rolled into a loaf, and baked. At night you might get a *Rotwein-Punsch* or a *Glühwein* which are a kind of mulled wine.

While Christmas Eve and Day are generally reserved for the family, visiting amongst friends often begins on the 26th and continues until New Year's Eve.

Coffee drinking is highly revered in Germany. The preparation, the drinking and the enjoying of a good cup of coffee is an art and a kind of afternoon ritual comparable to the Englisch "tea".

During a visit with an American family encamped near Mannheim the subject of coffee came up. This young dashing wife and her captain spouse had traveled all through Germany and looked in all of the various interesting nooks and corners, visited the Black Forest, Oberammergau and Hamburg, but had never been inside a Café-Konditorei. Our American wife said that someone in the States had said German coffee is bitter, black and tastes awful, and she had been afraid ever since to take the chance.

And what will be served then? Maybe *Heringssalat* or *Karpfen blau*, or some other favorite of the family, and possibly *Berliner Pfannkuchen* and *Glühwein*.

"Guten Appetit!"

Gisa v. Barsewisch

"Sometimes I was tempted," she said, "by all those wonderfully decorated cakes, but always I lost my nerve just before going in."

Well, you adventuresome Americans, have no fear. Go into the next coffeehouse you come to, possibly in mid-afternoon, and have a really good cup of coffee. Speaking as an American, I met the German cup of coffee head on with my eyes wide open and enjoyed it very much.

These coffeehouses over here are also one of the best examples of German "Gemüt-lichkeit". You can order one cup of that stuff and sit for hours if you want to. Write your letters, read your papers, discuss politics; no one will rush you or even expect you to drink a second cup unless you want to. In these shops you will also find assortments of cakes that you never dreamed of. Fruit cakes, layer cakes, fudge and nougat-filled cakes.

As it is heavily taxed, coffee here is much more expensive than in America, therefore a lot of trouble is taken when preparing it. The right amount of that brown powder is put into a little container with a piece of fil-

Wines: The Label Tells What's in the Bottle

ter paper which in turn is inserted into the elaborate coffee machine. Steam, boiling water and pressure force the best of the flavor out of the coffee into your cup. The coffee is brought to you hot, full of aroma and really good.

By this time you have been to the buffet and with trembling finger have already picked out a few pieces of butter creme layer cake with a portion of *Schlagsahne* (whipped cream — don't forget the *Schlagsahne*, nothing is complete without it). You now sit down and lean back. You breathe in the delectable aroma of the coffee. You add the right amount of sugar and, if you like, cream or condensed milk to suit your taste. Then comes the first sip. Do not attract attention to yourself but breathe in and sigh a little bit. Now you have broken the ice. Slowly and with much ritual you eat your cake and drink your coffee. When you have finished — relax.

Most Europeans still think that none of the pleasures of life should be rushed and that means especially drinking coffee.

A. S.

Germany's vineyards are situated in the northernmost wine growing regions of the world. Grapes ripen more slowly than elsewhere, but in years with favorable weather the result can be overwhelmingly good . . .

About six times more white wine than red is produced. All German white wines should be drunk cool but never ice-cold!

The main wine-growing regions are Rheingau, Rheinhessen, Mittelrhein, Pfalz, Moselle with Saar and Ruwer, Nahe, Ahr, Franken, Baden, and Württemberg. A rule of thumb: wines from the Moselle, Saar and Ruwer region come in green bottles, those from the Rhine region in brown ones, and Franken wines in low, fat bottles *(Bocksbeutel)*.

From the wine label one can learn the quality grade, year of vintage, district of origin or even the particular vineyard, and type of grape.

Here is an explanation of the quality designations:

Deutscher Tafelwein (German Table or Dinner Wine)

This group includes all so-called consumer wines, i. e. the lower price ranges. These wines can be mixed from several wines harvested in different locations of one larger wine-growing area. A name designating a special situation of vineyard (*Lage*) is not permitted on the label. However, details like the region, place name, kind of grapes and vintage year may be indicated if they apply to at least 75 per cent of the bottle content. Certain, officially defined improvements of the grape juice are permitted.

Qualitätswein bestimmter Anbaugebiete (Quality Wines from Certain Regions)

These are good wines of the medium price ranges. Quality wine must have been produced in one special wine-growing region.

Wines and Sekt (continued)

Labels must show an official control number. The kind of grapes used (Riesling, Sylvaner, Müller-Thurgau, Gewürztraminer, Burgunder etc.) must be indicated.

Minor, officially defined improvements of the grape juice are permitted. The prescribed minimum specific gravity of the grape juice lies higher than with table wines.

If a special situation of vineyard is indicated, this must apply to at least 75 per cent of the bottle content.

Qualitätswein mit Prädikat (Quality Wines with Distinction)

This is the top group of the quality wines. The wine must come from vineyards of equal situation within one special location, yielding grapes of the same quality and kind. No improvements allowed. Higher minimum specific gravity of the grape juice.

Distinctions: *Kabinett, Spätlese* (late harvested wine), *Auslese* (selected late harvested wine), *Beerenauslese* and *Trockenbeerenauslese* (raisin wines).

With regard to German champagnes, the following designations are used:

Schaumwein (Sparkling Wine)

The cheapest group, minimum alcohol content 70 grams per liter.

Qualitätsschaumwein or Sekt (Quality Champagne)

Label must show an official control number. Minimum alcohol content 80 grams/liter. Minimum storage time: nine months.

This quality may be called *Deutscher Sekt* (German champagne) if at least 60 per cent of the bottle content was made of German-grown grapes.

Deutscher Prädikatssekt (German Quality Champagne With Distinction)

The highest quality, having been produced from at least 75 per cent German grapes and complying with a number of further prescriptions regarding the quality of the grapes used, storage time, etc.

German Brandies, Gins etc.

According to German custom, a fine dinner is often topped with an after-dinner drink. To drink wine, beer or spirits by themselves after the meal is part of German social life.

While German wines and beers are reputed all over, the surprising variety of German *Schnaps* is little known abroad. German brandy, or *Weinbrand*, bears more resemblance in taste to bourbon whisky than to cognacs; German gin — of which *Steinhäger* is most popular, besides many variations, such as *Bommerlunder* and *Dornkaat* — is surely one of the world's best. Germans take their native liquor straight rather than mix it, and it is widely believed that this is a healthy way of drinking. But if you must, you can mix all your familiar vodka and gin drinks by using *Steinhäger* instead — in fact, Bloody Marys and Screwdrivers made with this German liquor have high quality; and *Weinbrand* will do in place of whisky when you are out for a Manhattan with German ingredients.

In addition to these two standard drinks of *Weinbrand* and *Steinhäger*, Germany offers

A Good Glass of German Beer

a plentiful choice of hard liquor made from bases other than grapes or grain and equally delicious. German fruit brandies include *Kirschwasser* distilled from cherries; *Himbeergeist*, from raspberries; *Erdbeergeist*, from strawberries; *Pflaumenwasser* and *Zwetschgenwasser*, from prunes and plums respectively; *Wacholder*, from juniper berries and *Enzian*, from gentian, that lovely flower of the Alps. You inhale their distinctive aroma before you sip them. And do not trust them; despite their bucolic basis, they are more powerful than they seem at first.

Written records from 6,000 years ago indicate that beer was brewed and drunk in what is often referred to as the cradle of mankind, Mesopotamia. Although the "beer" enjoyed by the Assyrians and the Babylonians bore little resemblance to the beer drunk today, its basic ingredients were as natural as those used today in Germany.

Purity — Important Since the Age of Columbus

Even today, German brewers adhere to laws, which determine the natural ingredients of beer, dating back to the time of Columbus. In 1516, the Bavarian Duke William IV enacted a brewing law, known to this day as the "German Beer Purity Regulation", which allows only the use of hops, malt, yeast, and water in the brewing of beer. This regulation forms the basis of the present beer tax law which still forbids any further additives to beer brewed in West Germany.

It is only since 1987, as a result of the standardization of European Community guidelines, that brewers from other EC countries whose beers do not meet the strict standards set by German tax authorities have been allowed to sell their beers in West Germany. These beer brewers, however, must clearly mark their different ingredients, such as malt substitutes or the use of chemicals, on the labels.

"A Basic Food"

In some regions of Germany, beer has been regarded as a "basic food" for centuries. It follows only coffee as the preferred beverage of all sections of the German population. While many poems have been written praising the virtues of wine, Germans average only 21 liters of wine a year. In contrast, Germans over the age of 15 drink on average 180 liters of beer a year. They are joined by nearly 15 million tourists from all over the world, including more than two million American visitors each year.

Germans Drink the Most Beer

Nowhere in the world is so much beer drunk as in the Federal Republic of Germany. While the Belgians, Czechs, Austrians, and New Zealanders follow closely behind, the average American consumes

German Beer (continued)

only about half as much beer as the German, even though the biggest brewery in the world, Anheuser Bush, produces almost 76.1 million barrels in the United States every year. That is nearly as much as the approximately 1,200 breweries in Germany produce all together.

Brewing — A Craft Aided by Nature

For brewing, first of all barley must be specially processed to produce malt. It is cleaned and sorted and then soaked in water for two days. The right temperature combined with plenty of oxygen brings about germination. To stop the germination process, the green malt is kilned (roasted) by raising the air temperature. It depends on the humidity, temperature and kilning time whether a light or dark malt (that is a Lager or dark beer) is produced as well as how strong the malt flavor will be.

Malt from the storage silos of the breweries is milled according to demand. It is then mixed with water. The mash obtained is subsequently heated to different temperatures. This causes the various components of the malt grain to liquefy. Next the insoluble starch of the barley grain is extracted by malting and mashing and converted into fermentable sugar enzymes thereby releasing protein, vitamins, and aroma substances. The percentage of the malt extracts, called the sweet wort, determines the calculation of the beer tax.

This wort is then separated from the spent grains, which are sold as high-quality animal food. The sweet wort is transferred into the brewing copper and, while hops are added, it is boiled for $1\frac{1}{2}$ hours. Through water vaporization, it acquires the desired concentration and absorbs the aromatic substances of the hops. The wort must still be clarified and cooled before fermentation can start. In the whirlpool, which is a vertical, cylindrical tank, protein particles and hops residues are removed.

The purified wort is cooled in heat exchangers and then poured into the fermentation vessels. After adding yeast, a natural biological process converts the malt sugar into alcohol and carbon dioxide.

Beer in this phase is still not ready for consumption. The "young beer", as brewers now call it, must go through a secondary fermentation and maturation for several weeks. This takes place in storage tanks, where the young beer accumulates carbon dioxide naturally and matures until it achieves a more refined flavor. Secondary fermentation takes place under pressure so that carbon dioxide is dissolved in the beer. Before the beer is bottled or poured into barrels, it is filtered, ensuring that the final product is crystal clear.

More Than 4,000 Different German Beers

While the largest German brewery, the Hamburg Holsten Brauerei, produces some 3.6 million hectoliters of beer annually, the bulk of the German brewing industry is made up of medium-sized companies.

Smaller breweries run by monasteries (*Klosterbräu*) still exist in Germany today, too. The nuns and monks offer their special beers primarily in their local beer gardens and monastic taverns. There are also smaller breweries owned by pubs who brew their own beers, often prized specialties, exclusively for their clientele.

All together, the consumer can choose from more than 4,000 different beers brewed by German breweries.

A Multitude of Varieties to Suit All Tastes

To distinguish the different types of beers, they are classified according to the guidelines set out by the tax authorities. The type of yeast used in brewing plays an important role here.

"Bottom-fermented" beers such as *Pils, Export, Lager,* or *Märzen* (brewed in March, *März*), which must be matured and cannot be served before autumn, on the occasion of Munich's Oktoberfest, for example, form the most important group.

German *Pils* is liked all over the world. It enjoys a market share of more than 50 per cent in West Germany and is the most popular beer in the Federal Republic. *Pils* also constitutes the main share of the total export of almost 5. 5 million hectoliters of German beer, of which 1. 3 million hectoliters are exported to the US today. *Pils* is a delicately bitter, tangy, strongly-hopped beer with a firm head which needs to be tapped with special care.

Export beer is also a light, but full-bodied beer which must, in accordance with the law, contain at least 12. 5 per cent sweet wort, equivalent to an alcohol content of about 4. 2 per cent. This type of beer, which can be transported relatively well over greater distances, actually bears the wrong name, because, in contrast to *Pils,* it is rarely exported anymore. —

Lager beers are also well known. Originally this name was used for beers which could be stored for a long time in the event you couldn't brew fresh beer because of summer temperatures. *Lager* is the most popular beer in Bavaria.

Even the strong beers — usually called *Bock* or ending with the syllable *-ator* — belong to the bottom-fermented beers. They have a strong malt aroma and are full-bodied because of their high content of sweet wort — at least 16 per cent.

These beers have an alcoholic content of more than 5. 5 per cent. The *Doppel-Bock* beers contain even more than 6 per cent alcohol, which an inexperienced beer drinker will soon notice.

Beer brewed with the help of bottom-fermenting yeast can be stored longer. The yeast needs a temperature of between 4 and 9 degrees Celsius to work. That is why in former centuries beer could only be brewed in winter and had to be stored in deep cellars until the German engineer Carl von Linde invented refrigeration machines in 1873.

In contrast, the yeast of "top-fermented" beer needs temperatures of between 15 and 20 degrees Celsius. After the brewing process is completed, the yeast which has floated up to the top is skimmed off. The yeast can be used again as an individual culture, because it regenerates.

The Lower Rhine specialty, the dark *Alt,* is of this type. Contradicting its name, *Alt* (old) beer should be drunk as young as possible.

Kölsch beer, which may only be brewed by

German Beer (continued)

24 breweries in Köln, is a top-fermented beer, but with a light color and with a strong flavor of hops.

Weizenbier, once a typical Bavarian specialty, now drunk all over West Germany, is produced in a special way. Not only is some malt made from wheat used in addition to the usual barley malt, but after brewing, *Weizenbier* is immediately poured into bottles together with its yeast components which allows the beer to continue to mature until its alcoholic content reaches about 4 per cent. It is then drunk as a very refreshing beverage from tall, half-liter conical glasses. There is also a clear *Weizenbier* in which the yeast is filtered out before the beer is bottled.

Low-Calorie Beers, Too

German beer contains all the nutrients, in liquefied form, which man needs to sustain his life. Enjoyed in moderation, beer is healthy — a fact acknowledged by doctors and appreciated by all those who like to drink it. For dieters and weight-conscious epicures, there are low-calorie beers with no alcohol or a maximum content of 1. 5 to 2 per cent. These beers have enjoyed increasing popularity among women, drivers, and sportsmen in recent years.

Modern Techniques Support a Venerated Craft

A little over 92 million hectoliters (approximately 2,430 million gallons) of beer are brewed in West Germany annually. Of this amount, about 25 million hectoliters are poured into barrels, tapped and served at the bar. More than 70 per cent of the total output of German breweries, however, is bottled or canned. The fully automatic machines in the big breweries can fill more than 100,000 bottles or cans per hour. It is indeed rare to find a brewery in Germany today whose production is not controlled electronically or whose storage tanks are not automated.

While the adoption and adaptation of modern technologies and techniques is essential, even today the successful production of a good beer depends on the personal skills of the master brewer. The art of brewing continues to be a most venerated craft.

200 Kinds of Bread — and 1,500 Types of Sausage

The Germans — in spite of all the changes that have taken place in their way of living and way of eating in recent years — are still great bread eaters. They eat bread not only for breakfast but also for supper (called *Abendbrot* — evening bread) and for in-between meals. There are some 200 different kinds of bread in Germany, 30 kinds of rolls (*Brötchen, Semmel*), and no less than 1,200 different kinds of pastries!

The Main Types of German Bread:

Weissbrot and Toastbrot

similar to the standard bread in the U. S., Canada and Britain — but not the standard bread of the Germans, which is:

Feinbrot or Mischbrot (Graubrot)

made from a mixture of wheat (*Weizen*) and rye (*Roggen*) flour, and

Vollkornbrot (Schwarzbrot)

made from whole rye or rye-and-wheat grains that are cracked or rough-ground. Many varieties from medium-brown to very darkbrown.

Mehrkornbrot

multi-grain bread, i. e. made of wheat, rye and even barley or oats.

Pumpernickel

a special type of very dark bread, made of rye groats and whole flour, baked at extremely low temperatures.

Knäckebrot

brittle rye bread thinly sliced.

Not only are the varieties of bread, rolls, pretzels, cakes and cookies immense, there are also large differences from town to town. The best advice we can give is to go to the nearest German baker's shop and try out what they have to offer.

Sausages

Naturally, Germans do not like their bread plain — and here is where the sausages come into play.

There are more than 1,500 different kinds of German sausage — raw, boiled, and smoked, seasoned in all sorts of ways, shaped in all kinds of forms.

Regional and local variety is immense, not only in recipes but also in names, so that here again the best advice is to make your own discoveries (don't hesitate to ask for a small quantity, such as *hundert Gramm*).

Here are the most important kinds of sausage:

Mettwurst (ground pork sausage)
coarse, medium and fine

Leberwurst (liverwurst)
pork or veal, coarse and fine

Blutwurst/Rotwurst (blood wurst)
meat (pork) and blood

A Confusing Variety of Milk Products

Sausages (continued)

Fleischwurst (kind of bologna)
beef, pork and veal

Bratwurst
pork sausage for frying, normal size or
very small

Wiener Würstchen — wieners.

Weisswurst (see page 55), *Bierschinken*,
Fleischkäse and *Leberkäse* (meatloaf) are
especially popular in Bavaria.

As for those *Wursts* sold at fast food snack
bars, see page 40.

Eat-by Dates

The following words are especially important to know for the foreign consumer in
Germany:

Verfallsdatum = expiration date after
which product may not be sold or consumed

mindestens haltbar bis . . . = minimum
time of storage, minimum validity date

verbrauchen bis spätestens . . . = use before

Datum siehe Deckelprägung = for date see
cap

Zutaten = ingredients

Why not try the one or the other of those
delicious milk products offered in German
shops today? Here's a short guide through
the confusing variety of labels and names:

Markenmilch — "branded milk" — is the
most widely consumed kind. Fat content:
3.5 per cent. Pasteurized and homogenized. Keeps well for several days in the
refrigerator.

Fettarme Milch — like above, but lower fat
content (1.5 — 1.8 per cent).

Magermilch — skimmed milk, hardly any
fat at all.

Vorzugsmilch — raw milk with 4.5 — 5
per cent fat content. Sours quickly.

H-Milch — homogenized milk, pre-
heated. Keeps at least six weeks when un-
opened. Special taste.

Buttermilch — buttermilk, by-product of
butter-making. Low in fat content. Keeps
for 7 to 10 days.

Schlagsahne — whipped cream (30 per
cent fat).

Crème fraîche — *sour cream (30 per cent
fat).*

Quark — similar to small curd cottage
cheese, offered with various fat contents.

The cheese variety in German shops is also
quite overwhelming.

The fat content of cheeses can be learned
by roughly dividing the " % Fett i. Tr."
figure on the label by 2. "Fett i. Tr." means
"fat content in the absolutely dry cheese".
So if a cheese is labeled as "30 % Fett
i. Tr.", this means it has about 15 per cent
fat content.

Among the most popular cheeses in Germany are *Emmentaler, Brie, Gouda,
Edamer,* and *Camembert.*

Road and Rail Traffic

"Public transportation is fine in Germany — but driving . . . terrible, nerve-racking!" That is what Americans usually say about the traffic situation over here. "I returned my rented car on the second day because I saw my life endangered by those horrid drivers," an American tourist told an interviewer just recently.

The Speed Shock

The greatest shock to Americans is the speed at which Germans drive. With few exceptions, there is no speed limit on the big freeways, or Autobahns (which are toll-free). There is only a "recommended speed" of 130 km/h (approx. 80 miles/h); many drivers nowadays don't go over this limit, but some do, and they are the ones who terrify the slow drivers on the left (passing) lanes of the Autobahns, "tailgating" and sometimes even flashing their lights (which is illegal).

On highways and secondary roads outside towns, the speed limit is 100 km/h (62 mi.), in towns 50 km/h and sometimes, on larger streets, 60 km/h (look for the signs).

Speed limits are not so strictly enforced as in the United States. There are radar controls, but obviously not enough, and the fines imposed are too low to really frighten drivers out of going 10 or 20 km above the limit. Only in extreme cases is the driver's license taken away.

Traffic Can't Get Much Denser

Most Germans love their cars, as you can easily see from the good shape in which they keep them. Germans also keep their cars for more years than Americans usually do. To the younger generation, owning a car is now almost a matter of course, but this is a rather recent develop-

Road and Rail Traffic (continued)

ment. In 1960, there were only eight million passenger cars in West Germany, now there are 33 million! For a country as small as West Germany this means that traffic density is now much higher than in the U. S.

Except for the Autobahns, most overland roads are narrower here than in America. Some have high crowns, dangerous curves, and even cobblestones which are treacherous when wet.

The congested maze of European city streets presents many problems to the American driver. They are full of no-entry and one-way-street signs, and sometimes you may find yourself going in a circle several times before finding the one little street that leads to your destination.

The variety of vehicles on German roads is greater than in the United States. Not only must you watch out for bicycles, motorcycles, busses, and extra-large trucks, but there are also great varieties among ordinary passenger cars. As the car tax is fixed according to the cylinder capacity, some smaller cars are not strong enough to accelerate as quickly as the normal American car. Passing maneuvers, therefore, may take more time.

Stoplights

There is also a difference in the behavior at stoplights. When the red light changes to yellow, meaning "stay put until the green appears", most German drivers view it as a preliminary "go" signal and shoot off, sometimes barely missing those traveling in the other direction where the light is changing to red and who seem to understand their yellow light not as "stop" or "clear the intersection" but as "hurry up or you'll have to stop".

A flashing yellow light always means "Caution". Unless there's a green arrow pointing their way, cars waiting at a red light are not allowed to turn right, as is sometimes the case in America.

Pedestrians in Germany must wait for their green light before crossing even if there is apparently no traffic.

Drunken driving is a felony under German law, as is leaving the scene of an accident, passing illegally, making U-turns on Autobahns, and several other traffic offenses.

It is also important to know that wearing seat belts is mandatory and that children under 12 years of age must ride in the back seats of cars here.

Always Keep Alert!

Our general advice to American drivers in Germany: learn the traffic rules well, maintain a sufficient interval, and try to stay out of situations that call for fast braking. Watch out for zebra-stripe crosswalks, where pedestrians have the absolute right of way, and remember that at unmarked intersections traffic coming from the right has the right of way. Don't be overcautious either, but never take driving easy over here. Always keep alert!

Summer morning in Hamburg's downtown shopping district
(c) Urs F. Kluyver

Of all sports, soccer attracts by far the largest crowds in Germany. Scene from an international match at the Olympic stadium in West Berlin.

(c) ZEFA-Waldkirch

Baustelle, Seitenstreifen, Kriechspur ...

Some German Words
A Driver Should Know

Driving on hilly sections of the Autobahn, you may see the word *Kriechspur* once in a while. It means "creeping lane" and denotes an extra lane on the right intended especially for slow-moving trucks, which can only "creep" uphill and would otherwise hold up faster vehicles which can make the elevation more easily.

Sometimes, there are German explanations under the "Attention!" signs which foreigners may find hard to understand. Here are some translations:

Seitenstreifen nicht befahrbar — soft shoulders
Seitenwind — side wind
Fahrbahnschäden — damaged road surface
Rauch — smoke
Baustelle auf 15 km — construction lot for 15 km

If you wish to make a short stop on the Autobahn, you may drive into one of the parking places along the road which are announced by a sign that shows a white "P" on blue background. (The free lane right of the driving lanes is for emergency stops only). The sign *Rastplatz bitte sauberhalten* means "Please keep the rest area clean".

The word *Raststätte* stands for the large restaurant-gas station complexes on the Autobahns.

Before complicated traffic intersections, there are sometimes signs indicating several directions with the words *Bitte einordnen* above them. This means "Please move into the proper lane".

Einfädeln means "to thread in", i. e. to carefully merge into a traffic lane.

Parkscheibe

In many places, parking is permitted in clearly designated (meterless) areas from 30 minutes to 2 hours, depending on the location, if you place your own blue *Parkscheibe* on your dahsboard behind your windshield, clearly visible to any passing policeman or -woman and showing your time of arrival. These cardboard gadgets are available in stationery stores and department stores.

Mofas and Motorbikes: Lights On!

Motorized two-wheeled vehicles — including Mofas, Mokicks and light motorbikes — must have the headlight on both night and day.

Car Insurance, License Plates, Fahrschule

Who ran into whom? That's the big question! Liability insurance (Haftpflichtversicherung) is obligatory for all car owners in Germany. In case of an accident — we hope it never happens to you — try to get hold of a witness immediately.

In Germany, a car keeps the same license plate as long it is registered with the local traffic authority. The first group of letters on the plate stands for the town or district (HL = Hansestadt Lübeck).

Anybody wishing to obtain a driver's license (Führerschein) in Germany has to go to an authorized driver's school (Fahrschule) and has to undergo a written and a driving test with the traffic authorities. The minimum age is 18.

Another Traffic Hazard: Bicycles

Not all of these cyclists know the traffic rules . . . therefore, take care!

Always watch for bicycles before making a right turn around a street corner.

Americans coming to Germany will soon notice that the bicycle population is much greater over here than in the States, and that one sees people from two to ninety-two on bikes.

Be careful not to mistake the bicycle paths for sidewalks. In Germany quite often these special lanes are in better shape than the sidewalks, but don't walk on them — you might get hit from the rear. Always look before crossing one.

Children up to the age of eight must ride their bicycles on the sidewalk if there is no bicycle path. Adults must use the street in this case.

Car drivers must always watch out for bicycles before making a right turn around a corner. When passing cyclists, keep a safe distance and remember that they are not always aware of the traffic rules!

It is forbidden to park a car on a bicycle path, but the sides of many sidewalks can be used for parking if they have special signs.

When Driving in Germany . . .

. . . Don't Bump That Bumper

Germans can be very touchy about their cars. German courts have decided that one must absolutely avoid even touching another car when maneuvering in and out of parking spaces, let alone bump its bumper. German bumpers are not made especially strong; also there is no standard height required for bumpers as in the States.

. . . and Don't Lose Your Patience

Sunday drivers are fine — on the scenic route — but not on the Autobahn, and especially not in the passing lane. In Germany, as in the States, the left lane of a two-lane freeway is for passing only.

Although some German drivers ignore that rule, it is *generally forbidden to pass on the right on Autobahns*. Only when traffic is proceeding in both lanes and the left lane is moving not faster than 60 km/h (37.2 miles/h), are the cars in the right lane allowed to move ahead at a speed that does not exceed that of the left lane by more than 20 km/h (12.4 miles/h). When the traffic on the left lane has come to a standstill, the right lane may pass at the maximum speed of 20 km/h.

Emergency Calls on the Autobahn

In case of a breakdown or in case of an accident on the Autobahn, look for the little arrows near the top of the white posts lining the road. They'll lead you to the nearest emergency call box, which is never more than one km away. To use, merely lift the cover of the microphone completely (up to the stop); the Autobahn control will answer. Most of the operators speak English, and if not, say clearly *Panne* for a breakdown, or *Unfall* for an accident; *Verletzte* are injured persons. Your location, *Standort*, is printed under the speaker at the very bottom of the box; also give the direction of the Autobahn such as "Kassel—Frankfurt".

— and on the Highway:

Many *Bundesstraßen* (federal highways) are equipped with emergency telephones, too. Watch for the sign with the telephone symbol and the word *Notruf* underneath. When lifting the microphone cover you are directly connected to the nearest police station.

ADAC or AvD, by the way, correspond to what AAA is in the States.

A Path for Emergency Vehicles

If there is a traffic jam on the Autobahn, a path between the lanes must be kept open for emergency vehicles. On three-lane freeways it must be kept open between the left and the center lane.

May I Help You? — Kann ich helfen?

The following phrases may be helpful to know if you have car trouble or if you wish to help a German driver on the road (in case of accidents with injured persons, German law obliges you to help!):

Haben Sie eine Panne? = Are you having car trouble?

Kann ich Ihnen helfen = May I help you?

Ja, das ist sehr freundlich von Ihnen! = Yes, that is very kind of you.

Der Wagen springt nicht an = The car won't start.

Soll ich anschieben? = Do you want me to push?

Könnten Sie ihn mit anschieben? = Could you help push it?

Wir müssen das Auto anschleppen = We must tow the car.

Haben Sie ein Abschleppseil? = Do you have a tow rope?

Vielen Dank! = Thank you very much!

Anschieben — to push a car

If your car breaks down, your first obligation is to warn oncoming traffic. Put warning lights or triangles at a sufficient distance from the car to enable drivers approaching from the rear to react in time.

Taxi Language

A cab or taxi is called *die Taxe* or *das Taxi* in German. The cab driver is *der Taxifahrer.* Indicating the destination of your ride, you may say: *"Ich möchte zum Bahnhof, bitte"* (to the station, please) or *"zur Hauptstraße, bitte"* or *"zur Kaserne, bitte!"* (to the main street, to the barracks).

If you want him to stop, say *"Bitte halten Sie hier!"*

Taxi rates vary from town to town. Within one area, the rate may vary depending on the time of the day, the number of passengers and the luggage transported. The number of passengers a driver may take is limited by law.

Make certain you have enough Deutsche Mark in small denominations. Taxi drivers will probably accept dollar bills, too, but at a much less favorable rate than usual, to make up for the time and gasoline needed to have the banknotes exchanged. A 10 per cent tip is customary.

At the Gas Station

Volltanken, bitte!

In gas stations offering full service, the attendant who cleaned your window, checked the air pressure, etc. expects a tip.

You need not speak much at a self-service gas station (*SB = Selbstbedienung*), but at other stations you may have to use some German words:

To have your tank filled up, say *"Volltanken, bitte!"* You can also ask for 10, 20, etc. liters of gas = *"zehn, zwanzig Liter Benzin"*. Roughly, one gallon equals nearly four liters; therefore, ten gallons of gas would be about forty liters.

Ethyl is *Super*, unleaded is *bleifrei* in German. Leaded regular gasoline is no longer for sale at German filling stations, but leaded *Super* (ethyl) is, as well as unleaded *Super*.

To have the air pressure in the tires checked, ask for *"Reifendruck prüfen"* or, more colloquial, *"Luft nachsehen"*. Air pressure is not measured in pounds per square inch here but in *bar* (formerly AT). For example, 28 PSI is 1.9 *bar*, and 30 PSI is 2.1 *bar*.

Oil is *Öl* in German; the battery, *die Batterie*; the tire, *der Reifen*.

gas station — *die Tankstelle*

parts store — *das Ersatzteillager*

repair shop — *die Reparaturwerkstatt*

exhaust — *der Auspuff*

brake — *die Bremse*

spare wheel — *der Ersatzreifen*

hood — *die Haube*

clutch — *die Kupplung*

engine — *der Motor*

oil change — *der Ölwechsel*

wiper — *der Scheibenwischer*

light — *der Scheinwerfer*

gas cap — *der Tankdeckel*

carburetor — *der Vergaser*

distributor — *der Verteiler*

spark plug — *die Zündkerze*

ignition — *die Zündung*

Public Transportation

Living in a Germany city, you will soon notice that you can save a lot of time, gas and nerves by using public transportation. Berlin, Hamburg, and Munich have extensive subway systems, other cities have one or two subway lines. All have highly developed bus systems, and some still have streetcars.

Get to know the local public transportation system. There are variations from city to city in the prices, ticket zones, and in how tickets are bought and validated.

Subscription Tickets

A New Yorker, used to paying his fare each time he uses the subway, may wonder what the German system is like when he sees that some people apparently buy a ticket while others simply walk through the open gate. The explanation is *Zeitkarten* or *Sammelkarten*, *Monatskarten*, etc. (subscription tickets valid for a week, a month, etc.) which are used by regular customers. Never enter a subway without having a ticket — you may have to pay a fine. There are sometimes checks either in the trains themselves or at the exit gates.

Zeitkarten are also used for streetcars and buses. In Hamburg, Munich, and in the Ruhr region a practical system has been introduced under which the same ticket is valid for all means of public transportation — the subway, the city railway, street cars, buses, and even (in Hamburg) river boats and ferries.

Ticket Automats

Many subway stations only have ticket automats. Make sure, therefore, that you have enough coins to buy your ticket from an automat. It is not easy to understand the system of calculating fares, and the system varies from city to city. But a little time spent with deciphering the fare system will reward you with fast and efficient public transport.

Please Take My Seat

In the subway, streetcar, or bus, if there is no seat left and an elderly person comes in, considerate children or young people offer their seats, saying *"Bitte, nehmen Sie meinen Platz"* or simply *"Bitte schön!"* If a seat bears the sign *Schwerbeschädigte*, this means it is reserved for invalids.

die U-Bahn — subway/underground

die S-Bahn — city railway

die Straßenbahn — streetcar/tram

der Bus — bus

die Bushaltestelle — bus stop

die Fahrkarte — ticket

der Fahrplan — schedule

Riding the Train in Germany

Have you ever thought of traveling in Germany by train? The trains of the German Federal Railroads (Deutsche Bundesbahn, a government-operated organization) are fast, punctual, clean, comfortable and safe. Long-distance trains have good diners and sleeping cars. Special *Autoreisezüge* even carry their passengers' automobiles along. Here are a few tips.

Reading the Schedule

First the train schedule. In German train stations you'll find two large schedules prominently posted. One is marked *Ankunft*, the other *Abfahrt*. It's the second, yellow one you'll be interested in. It gives destinations, times of departures and so on. (Small train schedules can also be bought at any German train station).

There are several columns on the *Abfahrt* schedule, with the following headings:

Zeit (meaning "time of departure")

Zug Nr. ("train number")

Nach (meaning "to" — in other words, destination)

Gleis (track)

or *Bahnsteig* (platform).

Look down the *Nach* column for a train that's going where you are, at about the time you'd like to leave. Departure times are in the *Zeit* column; military time is used. Times of arrival are shown after the city of destination, in smaller numerals, in the *Nach* column.

Kinds of Train

The kind of train (not to be confused with class of travel) is important:

Those listed in black type are *Nahverkehrszüge*, which are more or less "milk trains" that stop at nearly every fence post. These you'll want to avoid unless your trip is a short one. It's best to stick with the trains marked in red.

The first of the "red" trains is the Eilzug (semi-fast). These trains are marked by an "E" before the train number. It's advisable to take an *Eilzug* for trips of 50 kilometers or less.

Next is the *D-Zug* and *Fern-Express*, marked with a "D" or "FD" before the train number. These long-distance trains are faster and make fewer stops than the "E"-trains, but for distances under 50 kilometers you pay a bit extra — 3 marks, a so-called *Zuschlag* (supplement). You get a separate ticket for the *Zuschlag*, which you can buy with your regular ticket at the window, or from the conductor on the train (but this costs extra).

A new type, which is gradually replacing the D-Zug system, began to operate in the fall of 1988: these *Interregio* trains connect Germany's medium-sized centers at two-hour intervals.

The *Interregio* schedule is combined with that of the *Intercity* (IC) system which has been in existence for many years. IC trains are comfortable and very fast long-distance trains that whiz through most smaller towns. But again, you pay extra for the fast service and comfort. The *Zuschlag* is 6 marks for both 1st and 2nd class (including seat reservation — *Platzkarte*).

Over 200 *Intercity* trains link all major

German cities all over the country at one-hour intervals between 7 a. m. and 11 p. m., thus offering fast and highly comfortable transportation between city centers. There are numerous connections between the individual lines, and as a rule passengers need only cross the platform to change trains.

Those IC trains that travel beyond the borders of the Federal Republic are called *EuroCity* (EC).

✱

But back to reading the schedule:

The number in the last column of the departure schedule, *Gleis* or *Bahnsteig*, shows which track or platform your train leaves from.

Departure schedules also have a number of symbols pertaining to trains, some of which are important. If there's any small print under the time in the *Zeit* column of the train you're interested in, it's best to inquire at *Information* (*Auskunft*). It probably has to do with times when the train will or will not run.

Several different symbols are used in the *Nach* column. Crossed knife and fork, as might be expected, means the train has a dining car — called *Speisewagen*. The symbol of a wine glass means that food and drink are available on the train, probably sold by vendors who wander through the cars. (In the first class cars of IC trains, conductors even serve drinks and little snacks right in the compartment).

A bed means, obviously, that the train has a sleeping car (*Schlafwagen*, wagon-lit). A smaller symbol, supposed to represent a couch, means that the train has a car or cars convertible for sleeping purposes, *Liegewagen* (couchettes). You don't change clothes in these cars, sexes are not separated, and you get only a blanket and a pillow. The supplement is much cheaper than for a *Schlafwagen*. If you plan to use either a *Schlafwagen* or a *Liegewagen* be sure to make a reservation when you get your ticket, especially in the holiday seasons.

If you have any question at all about your train, see *Auskunft*, Information. People in this office will go to great lengths to help you get where you're going.

Buying the Ticket

Buy your ticket at any *Reisebüro* (Travel Office) in advance or directly at the train station (although in this case you should have ample time, as the modern, computerized ticket machines take longer than you would think). Look for the sign *Fahrkarten-Inland. Fahrkarte* means ticket. *Inland* means what you'd suppose. If you want a ticket to go outside Germany, go to a counter marked *Ausland.*

To ask for a ticket, simply say *nach . . . bitte* — wherever you're going. If you don't speak German, it might be best to write your destination on a slip of paper and show it to the person behind the window.

If your ticket is to be one-way, add the word *einfach*, which means literally "simple". If you want a roundtrip, say *hin und zurück,* which means *"there and back".* You can also say *Rückfahrkarte*. For round-trips that cover a certain minimum distance and include a weekend, sizable reductions may be possible — just ask at the nearest travel office (*Reisebüro*) or train station. To reserve a seat, ask for a *Platzkarte*.

Riding the Train (continued)

EURAIL-PASS and Other Reductions

There are also various reductions for groups (beginning with two people) and favorable package trips for city tours and short vacations. Large reductions (of usually 50 per cent) are possible for holders of a *Senioren-Pass* (for women over 60 and men over 65), a *Junioren-Pass* (for young people from 18 to 22 or 26 for students, a *Taschengeld-Pass* for those from 12 to 17, *Eurail* and *Interrail* passes. A piece of good advice: When planning a visit to Europe, U. S. tourists should buy a EURAIL-PASS well before leaving the United States; it offers unlimited first class train travel in 16 European countries for 7, 15 or 21 days and for one, two or three months. EURAIL Youth Passes are valid one or two months. Members of foreign NATO forces in Germany and their dependents can also buy the EURAIL-PASS over here at some large train stations — at small stations it can be ordered.

The DB Tourist Card, valid four, nine or 16 days for unlimited mileage, is a very good deal for foreigners who want to see a lot of Germany in a short time.

Group Travel

In addition, the following reduced fare plans are particularly interesting:

Group travel: Reduced rates for six or more passengers. Lowest rates are during low season and non-holiday periods. Apply at least seven days before your departure date.

Familien-Pass: This DM 130 pass offers half-price travel on German trains for one year to all members of one family. Children must be under 18, unmarried and living in the same household. If an adult is traveling, at least two persons must go together, but one child can travel alone.

U. S. School Study Trips:

Special one- to seven-day trips are offered for American Dependent Schools in the Federal Republic of Germany. For detailed information, ask your host nation teacher.

Classes of Trains

What about classes of trains? There are only two, first and second. The first is plushy and costs 50 per cent more than second class.

Checking Baggage

To check baggage at a station temporarily, go to a window marked with a whopper of a word: "*Gepäckaufbewahrung*". *Gepäck* means baggage. Many stations now have lockers (*Schließfächer*). If you use these, be sure to pay the extra amount required if you plan to check your bag longer than the stated maximum.

Should you wish to check baggage on your ticket, go to a window marked "*Reisegepäck*".

A restaurant will usually be available in the station — often two: first and second class. They have nothing to do with the class of ticket you have: it's simply that the layout and fare of the first-class restaurant will be a bit fancier.

Larger train stations have facilities for everything from exchanging money to buy-

(continued on page 80)

Some Railroad Words in Short

The train schedule (Fahrplan) is easy to find in the station (Bahnhof). It is marked with "Ankunft" (arrival) and "Abfahrt" (departure). "Zeit" means time of departure; "Nach" means to, i. e. the destination; "Zug Nr." is the train number, "Gleis" is track; and "Bahnsteig" is platform.

"Fahrkarten" means tickets. Simply say "nach . . ." — wherever you are going. For oneway, add "einfach", roundtrip is "hin und zurück" or "Rückfahrkarte". For D, FD, IC and EC trains you pay a supplement (Zuschlag). To reserve a seat, get yourself a "Platzkarte".

"Gepäckaufbewahrung" is the place where you can check baggage at a station temporarily. "Gepäck" means baggage. To check baggage on your ticket, go to a window marked "Reisegepäck". "Annahme" is where they accept your baggage. "Ausgabe" is where you get it back. Lockers are called "Schließfächer" in German.

Riding the Train (continued)

ing toothpaste. Many have automats that dispense such items as shaving cream, stockings, and candy bars.

At the Platform

About ten minutes before your train is due to depart, go to the platform.

Platforms and tracks are clearly marked by number. On your platform there's likely to be a sign giving the destination and time of departure of your train. Check this sign to confirm that you're where you should be.

German trains usually run on schedule. Late trains are announced over a P. A. system, and there's the usual amount of garbling normally connected with train announcements. When you hear an announcement, listen for your destination, the train number, or the time of departure. The expression in German for being late is *"Verspätung haben"* — literally "to have lateness" — or *"der Zug verspätet sich um . . . Minuten"*. On small or medium-sized stations, the fast trains stop often for only one or two minutes. Only in the large towns are the stops a little longer.

Classes of cars are pretty prominently marked "1" or "2" so you'll know which is which. Check also to see whether your car is a *Raucher* (smoker) or a *Nichtraucher* (nonsmoker). Some cars are half and half.

Some overland trains combine cars with different destinations for part of the trip, which may be disconnected at a certain station and added to other trains. You ought to check whether the car bears the right destination on the outside before entering it; there are also signs in the cars themselves. If you have a *Platzkarte* with a car number, look for the *Wagenstandanzeiger* (a graphic plan showing the order of the cars in the train) on the platform to see where your car will stop.

In the Train

Train etiquette calls for you to greet the occupants in the compartment upon entering (*Guten Tag*) and to ask whether a seat is occupied before you sit down. The usual question is, *"Ist dieser Platz noch frei?"* It's also common to say goodbye (*Auf Wiedersehen*) to other occupants when you leave. Your ticket will be punched once or twice

while you are on the train. The conductor may ask for *Fahrtausweise*, or he may use the expression *"Ist noch jemand zugestiegen?"* which means "Has anyone here boarded since tickets were last checked?"

German trains, like other European trains, have no drinking water. (The water from the faucet in the lavatory is not drinkable). If you're thirsty, try to catch a vendor selling bottled drinks.

As for restroom facilities, you'll find them at the end of each car. There are no separate facilities for men and women. The sign on the door will say *"Toilette"* or "WC". The sign near the handle of the door of the *Toilette* will tell you whether the room is occupied (*besetzt*) or free (*frei*).

Except for IC trains, stops are not announced in the train, but over loudspeakers in the station. It's a good idea to have checked the schedule and know about when you'll arrive at your destination. Stations themselves are pretty well marked with large signs. *Hbf* stands for *Hauptbahnhof* (main station).

Gute Reise!

The Mail and the Phone

A Multitude of Services

You've probably seen its bright yellow deposit boxes and trucks with their distinctive post horn symbol. The German Federal Postal System *(Bundespost)* is pretty hard to ignore; its facilities are everywhere. The local *"Post"* or *"Postamt"* (post office) is an important place not only for the German citizens of the community but also for tourists from abroad or foreigners living on the German economy. They should know, therefore, that besides performing what Americans think of as normal postal services, the *Bundespost*

— owns and operates West Germany's telephone and telegraph systems (facilities for both are available at local post offices) as well as the *Telex* and *Datex* services

— owns or controls the equipment for West Germany's radio and television networks

— offers banking services — both savings and checking accounts (through local post offices)

— offers subcriptions to newspapers and magazines.

Following are some tips on how to use the local German post office.

Telegrams

Except for the fact that you send telegrams from the post office rather than Western Union, the system is much the same as in the States. You merely put your message on a form, available at the post office, and take it to the counter. You can also phone in a telegram.

A mailgram, or letter telegram, is called *"Brieftelegramm"* in German.

Telephone

Telephone calls to anywhere in the world can be placed at a German post office. Simply go to the counter marked *"Telefon"* or *"Fernsprecher"* and give the operator the number you want. She'll place the call and direct you to a booth to take it. You may be asked to pay a deposit before the call; the final bill you pay afterward.

More than likely, however, you'll do your public phoning from a (Bundespost-owned) booth. There are two kinds of booth. One is for local calls only. A single call costs three 10-Pfennig pieces (for eight

The Mail and the Phone (continued)

minutes). If you want to call German Information, the word to look for on the cover of the phone book is "*Auskunft*". Most information operators speak some English.

The other kind of booth pay phone is for local and long distance calls. It is larger and has coin slots for 50-Pfennig and 1-Mark pieces as well as a 10-Pfennig slot. Using it you can call anywhere in Germany, and even abroad from some phone booths. You have to know the area code prefix (*Vorwahl*), of course, which you can get from a list placed on the wall next to the phone or from *Auskunft*. For a long-distance call you deposit your 30 or 50 Pfennige or more, dial straight through, begin talking, and then drop in more money, each time the sign "*Sprechzeit zu Ende*" (speaking time is up) lights. If you want a distant military number, you dial the code first, then the military prefix of the area, then your number.

During the hours 6 p.m. to 8 a.m. there is a cheaper rate for direct-dial long-distance calls. The night rate also applies on Saturdays and Sundays as well as on most German holidays.

For private phones, the cost per call unit is 23 Pfennigs. The duration of a call for local calls is limited to eight minutes (twelve minutes for the night rate).

More about telephoning on pages 84 to 86.

Buying Stamps

As a rule, stamps can only be bought in a post office or from stamp vending machines outside post offices or elsewhere in the town. Frequently, shops selling picture postcards also have stamps available.

Letter and Card Service

Letter and card service is much the same as in America (but faster).

Normal letters to German destinations and all letters and cards to European countries, including Turkey and Russia, automatically go airmail without additional charge.

Airmail letter rates to other foreign countries vary. It's best to check at the counter. There are also special rates for printed matters (*Drucksachen*).

You can send a letter or postcard (or *Päckchen*, discussed later) by registered mail. Just say, "*Einschreiben, bitte*". And you can have a letter or postcard sent by special delivery (*Eilboten*).

The German word for stamp, by the way, is *Briefmarke* or, officially, *Postwertzeichen*.

Postleitzahlen

Germany also has zipcode numbers (*Postleitzahlen*). A booklet listing them is available at the post office. In the address the German zip code comes before the name of the city. If you know the number of the delivery post office (used in large communities only), put it after the name of the city. This is what the letter address should look like:

Herrn (Frau or Fräulein)
Dr. H. Schmidt
Schulzstraße 35
5300 Bonn 1

Note that the name of the street comes before the street number. The return address should be written into the left upper corner of the envelope's front. — For international mail between most European countries, it is sufficient to add the letters used to identify the "nationality" of cars to the zip code:

D 5300 Bonn.

For c/o your write *per Adr.* in German letter addresses, or, for persons living with a German family, *bei* (*bei Schmidt*). *Zu Hd. von* or *z. Hd.* means Attn. (Mr. X).

Parcels

There are two classes of package, the *Paket* and the *Päckchen*. The *Paket* is a normal package, sent by parcel post methods, the rate depends on the weight and the distance. In addition to the address on the package itself, a separate card (*Paketkarte*) must be filled out. Each ordinary parcel is insured up to 500 DM. Additional insurance may be had for a fee (called *Wertgebühr*). The delivery service charges a fee for each package delivered, unless the sender has paid this charge at the time of mailing.

If your package is small, ask if it will go as a *Päckchen*. A *Päckchen* is forwarded like a parcel, but at a much cheaper rate. No *Paketkarte* is required for it. For *Päckchen* to foreign countries you will, however, have to fill out a small green customs declaration.

If you want rush service on a package, send it as a *Schnellsendung* (within the Federal Republic) or as a *dringendes Paket* (to foreign countries).

Postal Money Orders

The *Zahlkarte* is the pale blue form used for paying money into a postal account (*Postgirokonto*).

The pink *Postanweisung* is used if the money is to be paid by the postman in cash directly to an individual or firm.

The *Auslandspostanweisung* is an international money order. You pay German marks, and the recipient of the payment receives cash in the currency of the country.

Eurocheques, American Express traveler's cheques, and DM traveler's cheques of German financial institutions may be cashed at all post offices with the "ec" symbol during normal hours (bring your passport along).

Large German post offices are so set up that the various counters are specialized with regard to their services; each has a sign over it telling what it handles.

If you have any questions about how to use German post office services, ask at the counter. There will usually be someone on hand who speaks some English. Or, if you know some German, get a little yellow booklet, called *Postgebührenheft*, at the post office. It contains detailed information.

For Stamp Enthusiasts:

Stamp collectors who want to make sure that they get all new German stamps can subscribe and have the new stamps sent every three months. Pick up and fill out a form at the post office, or write to:

Versandstelle für Sammlermarken
Mainzer Landstraße 187—189
6000 Frankfurt 1

or to:

Versandstelle für Sammlermarken
Goethestraße 2
1000 Berlin 12.

Telephone Language

When answering the phone, whether at home or in the office, it is customary in Germany to give one's family name, although it is no longer considered impolite to answer with a simple "Hallo". Asking to be transferred to someone else, the caller may say: "Guten Tag, hier ist Meier, könnte ich bitte Herrn Müller sprechen?"

"Schmidt & Co., Guten Tag!"
Company operators often answer calls with an additional "Guten Tag" or "Grüß Gott". When transferring a call, they will say: "Moment (Augenblick), bitte" or "ich verbinde" (I'll transfer you).
"Bitte, bleiben Sie am Apparat!" means "hold on, please!"

The official word for telephone is "Fernsprecher", but everyone says "Telefon". The word for phone booth is "die Telefonzelle".
The sign "Fasse dich kurz!" in phone booths means "Make it short!"
Paying three 10-Pfennig-coins, you can telephone locally for eight minutes.

More About Telephoning

Calling from the Hotel

Many an American tourist in Germany gets a shock when he or she is presented with the hotel's "outrageous" telephone bill. German hotel managers insist that their high telephone rates (some charge three times the normal rate) are no "rip-off" but that they need the money to make up for the costs of installing and maintaining the complicated self-dialing equipment.

For calls to the U. S., a possible way-out of the dilemma is explained below.

Looking for "Operator"?

Except for company and hotel phone operators, the ever-present, helpful operator of the U. S. phone system does not exist in Germany. The German telephone network is fully automatic so that you can dial all your inland calls yourself. You can also dial calls to some 139 countries outside Germany directly from any private phone, many hotel phones, and from a few public pay phones (you will find such special booths, marked with a green sign, at the airports, for instance).

First of all, you dial the country code (001 in the case of the States), followed immediately by the code for the desired local network area, and lastly the subscriber's call number.

Town Codes and Phone Numbers

Germany has no area codes, but town codes instead. They all begin with a zero (0) and can have from two to four digits after that.

German local phone numbers are not all seven-digit numbers, they may have as little as three, or up to eight digits. They are separated from the town codes by either a slash (/) or by putting the town code in parentheses. If you are looking for a phone number in a town other than the one you are in, call the telephone information *of the town you are in* (always No. 1188), they have lists for all towns in Germany.

Charge Units of DM 0,23

Accounting is performed in charge units of DM 0,23 according to the duration of the call and the country in question (the inland rate applies to all EC countries and others bordering on the Federal Republic). A selfdialled call to anywhere in the U. S., including Hawaii and Alaska, presently costs you 9,43 Marks for three minutes.

Under the German system there is no telephone calling card or credit card. Also, your VISA or MasterCard etc. cards are not accepted by phones (with the exception explained below). You can, however, buy a "Telefonkarte" at a post office and use it with special telephones (found at post offices, airports, railroad stations, etc.) until the amount you have paid is used up.

Telephone Calling Cards

And *for calling the U. S., there is an important exception:* If you have a valid VISA or MasterCard issued by a U. S. bank, you can obtain an AT&T card (by calling toll free 0130-9869, ext. 174). Holding this card, you can call the U. S. directly under 0130-0010 (toll free). You will talk to an AT&T operator in the U. S. who places your call (it may take from 5 to 30 seconds for the operator to answer). This makes it possible to call collect or to charge the call

More About Telephoning (continued)

to your credit card. The service can also be used for directory assistance.

Note: If you have a private phone in Germany, your monthly phone bill will indicate, in the column *Anzahl der Gebühreneinheiten*, not the number of phone calls you made but the number of charge units (which is one per local call of eight minutes but may be 10 or 20 or more for long-distance calls). Twenty charge units per month are included in the minimum monthly fee of DM 27 per telephone installed. There are no taxes added to telephone costs.

Itemized phone bills with number dialed, date and price for call have never been known here but may be introduced in the 1990s.

All the country-codes and the most frequently used town codes are to be found in the little yellow book that comes with the telephone directory. If you have any questions about numbers or codes, ring Information (often, the line is busy and you must wait): for national trunk calls: 1188, for international trunk calls: 00118.

If you need the help of a German operator, call 010 for inland and 0010 for abroad.

As there is normally no operator involved in the German telephone system, there are also no person-to-person calls possible, no collect calls (except at the expensive "operator-assisted rate"), and no calls can be charged to another number.

Some more expressions in connection with telephoning:

. . . am Apparat = . . . speaking

Die Rufnummer hat sich geändert = the number has been changed

Kann ich eine Nachricht hinterlassen? = Can I leave a message?

Wer spricht dort, bitte? = Who is speaking, please?

Entschuldigung, falsch verbunden or *Ich habe mich verwählt* = Sorry, wrong number

Auf Wiederhören = Good-bye (literally: hope to hear you again)

Emergency Calls

In most German communities, the police phone number for any emergency is 110, and the fire department and emergency first-aid service is usually reached by calling 112.

Some public telephone booths are equipped with a lever device that puts your emergency call right through with no need to dial or deposit coins.

Some words you may need when reporting an emergency:

fire — *Feuer*
hold-up — *Überfall*
accident — *Unfall*
with injured persons — *mit Verletzten*
burglary — *Einbruch*

German Isn't That Tough!

"I'd like to air a grievance", I said to Fritz, my German friend, the other day.

"And that is?" he asked.

"I think that the Germans shouldn't always contend that their language is so difficult."

"I beg your pardon!"

"I said I don't think Germans is so hard!"

"Na, sowas! (aghast). How can you say such a thing? Why the Germans themselves make mistakes even. And the grammar! (eyes cast upwards in awe). So-o-o difficult. First off, there's the problem of distinguishing between *mir* and *mich.* And then there's *der, die, das.* How could a foreigner possibly remember all that? And capitalization. And (breathless). . ."

"Stop, stop, stop — *bitte."*

"Bitte?!"

Please excuse me, dear reader, for interrupting him so abruptly, but this heated discussion on the difficulties of learning German could go on for hours! *"Die deutsche Sprache ist eine schwere Sprache",* my German friend Fritz claims.

He is not alone; most Germans entertain the very same thought. And I as an English speaking person, an American, disagree. Is the German language really so terribly difficult? Is it impossible for a foreigner to learn it, at least halfway fluently? I don't think so and here are a few of my reasons why.

In the first place, an English speaking person attempting to learn German unknowingly has put a few rounds of the battle behind him. Why? Because English and German are blood brothers. Both are divergences of the so-called Indo-European language, a prehistoric tongue from which many, many others have emerged. Anglo-Saxon, the first form of English, was a Germanic dialect. This was later strongly influenced by French.

Many Old Friends

Being two peas from the same linguistic pod, there should then be a great similarity.

The beginner doesn't have to delve deeply into the complexities of German before he begins to meet some very familiar looking

German Isn't That Tough! (continued)

words — *der Arm, die Hand, der Ball, das Gold, der Finger.* Philologists call these "perfect cognates" because the meaning and spelling are exactly the same. Nor does the beginner have to be a genius to see the similarity of the "near cognates" — *die Mutter, der Vater, das Bier, der Mann, die Maus, das Haus.* You'll be meeting hundreds of these two types of words throughout your study of German.

Fremdwörter

Sooner or later you'll stumble on another type of "old friend", and then a second, and a third and a fourth. Why, there seems to be no end of them. I'm talking about the *Fremdwörter,* the "foreign words", so called because they have crept into the German language through the centuries from other languages, without undergoing much "Germanization". Just a flip of the tongue to give the word "a German touch", and you have *die Explosion, die Nation, die Information, die Position, das Element, direkt, absolut, der Doktor* (of Latin extraction); *das Chaos, die Atmosphäre, das Drama, die Politik* (Greek); *das Manöver, die Parade, der Offizier, die Armee, der Moment*

(French); *der Moskito* (Spanish); *die Arie, das Stakkato* (Italian); *der Sport, der Flirt, boxen, der Jazz, das Handikap* (English).

If a German stumbles over a *Fremdwort,* don't smirk; some of the more difficult ones like *Psychologie* or *Meteorologie* are really hundred-dollar tongue twisters. In English, these same words present less of a problem. The American is more apt to glibly rattle them off; in a way his whole language is *fremd.* Several times in German history, attempts have been made to rout out these words — without much success.

A word of warning though; usually the meaning of these *Fremdwörter* correspond, but once in a while one trips you up. One good example that comes to my mind is the German *sensibel,* which has nothing in common with the English conception of the word. A *sensible Frau* is not a sensible woman, but a sensitive woman!

A Picture Language

Now, I'm afraid, the similarity ends. But there's another trick to learning the language, which German itself offers by its very make-up and which lends it a particu-

lar charm. German is a picture language. And the Germans themselves don't even realize it. As a child uses building blocks to construct houses and tunnels and buildings, German makes use of its simple words by putting two or three together — but there always remains a logical thread between the original word and the new.

From Stinktier to Fingerhut

One of my very favorite of these words is the German for skunk. This animal's most obvious characteristic is that it stinks. The Germans evidently thought so, too. They named it a *Stinktier* (*Tier* — animal). But what might they call a thimble? In your mind's eye picture a thimble on your finger. What does it look like? A hat perhaps? Sure — thimble in German is *Fingerhut,* a finger hat. The psychology of this word goes even deeper, for the English hat (an Anglo-Saxon word, and remember that was a Germanic dialect) and the German *Hut* derive from an old word "huot", which in one sense means protection. A hat protects your head from the outside elements, a thimble protects your finger from the prick of the needle. And further, *eine Hütte* (hut) is a little house giving shelter. To be *auf der Hut* means to be on your guard.

Because of the picturesqueness of German words, they can be easily remembered and a basic vocabulary is built up rather quickly.

Here are a few more picture words:

Volksmund	people's/mouth (vernacular)
Arbeitgeber	work/giver (employer)
Menschenfresser	human being/eater (cannibal)
Menschenfreund	human being/friend (philanthropist)
Blutarmut	blood/poverty (anemia)
Schirmherr	schirmen: to protect (patron)
Fallschirm	fall/umbrella (parachute)
Durchschnitt	through/cut (average)
Ausflug	out/fly (excursion)
Bildhauer	picture/cutter (sculptor)
Standbild	stand/picture (statue)
Neugier	new/eagerness avidity (curiosity)

Prefixes

There is still another possibility of word construction. This time your tools are — prefixes. Now, this sounds pretty dull — until you see how it is done. By adding various prefixes (for instance, *be-*, *ent-*, *aus-*, *über-*) to one basic word, whole new word groups are opened up — but here again, no matter how diverse or abstract, if you try you can still literally "see" the tie-in with the root. Let me show you the verb *führen* (to lead):

Young Bob plans to take out (*ausführen*) his girl friend Sally one evening. He is well-liked and the leader (*Anführer*) of his gang. Up to now he has never been introduced (*einführen*) to Sally's parents. He tries to behave very well (*sich gut aufführen*).

While waiting for Sally, Bob and her parents chitchat about this and that, his studies which he plans to pursue (*fortführen*), and then about trade, importing (*einführen*) and exporting (*ausführen*). The young couple plans that evening to see a performance (*Aufführung*) of a play. Later that evening he tells her how alluring (*verführerisch*) she looks. They plan to marry, but up to now they cannot talk her father into the idea. In secret they talk about a plan they are going to carry out (*durchführen*). They will simply elope (*entführen*).

Many Americans have said to me that they think German is a "funny" language. They don't mean this at all in a derogatory sense. Nor do I, when I say German has a certain simplicity, naiveness, and humor quite lacking in English. Knowing this, one can understand all the better why some Germans think English is a bit "sober".

It is impossible in one short article to illustrate all the quaintnesses of German, but let me, as an example, introduce a particular friend of mine. I don't quite know what to call him, for "he" is not really a he, or feminine or even neuter. He is a strange

German Isn't That Tough! (continued)

little character that runs around doing all sorts of things that no one else wants to do. He opens doors and closes them, he even sits down for whole groups, to mention only two of his many duties. He does have a name though — *man*. To go back to my two illustrations: in English "a door is opened or closed", but in German this strange little "mother's helper" goes to work — *"man macht die Tür auf"* or *"zu"*, or *"man setzt sich"* and a hundred people sit down. In English this *man* is usually translated, if at all possible, by "one" or "you" or even "it".

The Grammar Is Not That Bad

No mention has been made yet of one subject, a subject which surely only a grammarian could love, namely grammar. And with reason. It is too vast. But grammar is a necessary evil. How could you understand the insides of a car if you have not first taken it apart nut for bolt? Memorizing scads of rules is no fun. But once the rules of German grammar have been learned (there are really not too many of them and they are pretty much kept, contrary to English which only seems to "make 'em to

break 'em"), the game may not have been won but a touchdown surely has been scored.

I'd like to point out just one more thing before closing, a real booby-trap which the beginner constantly falls into head over heels: translating idiomatic phrases from one language into the other. Sometimes it works, but other times — well, just beware! One evening at a very elegant cocktail party, a young American lady said to a distinguished guest with whom she was holding a conversation, *"Wenn Sie nichts an haben, dann kommen Sie vorbei."* Dead silence, for this seemingly innocent remark "to come on over, when you've nothing on" proved a real conversation stopper. *"Nichts anhaben"* conveys in German unfortunately only one meaning — the state of undress!

I hope with these few illustrations and tips I've succeeded in making my point that German is not impossible to learn. Over 90 million people speak German, and they can't all be geniuses!

Carolyn LaRocque

Acquisitions From the English

German has taken over many words from English, but sometimes the meaning has changed. Here are some of the more recent acquisitions (with the German gender of the nouns in parentheses):

Band (jazz band) (f)	Killer (m)
Beat (m)	Live (broadcast)
Bestseller (m)	Make up (n)
Boss (m)	Mid-life crisis (f)
Comeback (n)	Outsider (m)
Computer (m)	Paperback (n)
Container (m)	Party (f)
Countdown (m)	Pipeline (f)
Design (n)	Playboy (m)
Disc Jockey (m)	Public Relations (f)
Do-it-yourself	Publicity (f)
Drink (m)	Sex (m)
Entertainer (m)	Show (f)
Fairplay (n)	Sit-in (n)
Feature (n)	Song (m)
Festival (n)	Story (f)
Gag (joke) (m)	Teach-in (n)
Happening (n)	Team (n)
Hit (musical) (m)	Teenager (m)
Hobby (n)	Thriller (m)
Image (n)	Trend (m)
Job (m)	Understatement (n)

Reading German Signs

Direction signs are good and practical — as long as you can understand them... Here are a few translations of German signs that you may find useful to know:

What do these signs mean?

Achtung!	watch out!
Anmeldung	Registration
Ausfahrt freihalten	Don't block the driveway
Ausfahrt	Exit (for cars)
Ausgang	Exit
Auskunft	Information
Betreten auf eigene Gefahr	Enter at your own risk
Bissiger Hund	Beware of the Dog (Dog bites)
Bitte klingeln	Please ring
Bitte nicht berühren	Do not touch
Drücken	Push (door)
Einfahrt	Entrance (for cars)
Eingang	Entrance
Eintritt verboten	No entry
Etage	Floor (as in 3rd floor)
Fahrstuhl	Lift, Elevator

Flughafen	Airport
Frisch gebohnert	Freshly waxed floor
Frisch gestrichen	Wet paint
Fußgänger	Pedestrians
Geöffnet	Open
Geschlossen	Closed
Hinten aussteigen	Get off at the rear
Hochspannung	High Tension
Kasse	Cashier
Keine Haftung	We take no responsibility (for objects deposited, etc.)
Kein Zutritt	No Entry
Lebensgefahr!	Danger to Life!
Nichtraucher or *Rauchen verboten*	No Smoking
Notausgang	Emergency Exit
Polizeiruf	Police Call
Reserviert	Reserved
Ruhe	Silence
Stadtmitte	City Center
Sprengstoff	Explosives
Tollwutgefahr	Danger: Rabid Animals in Area
Vorsicht	Caution
ziehen	Pull (door)

Sprechen Sie Englisch? — Do You Speak German?

Here are a few phrases of "small talk" that you may find useful to know when opening a conversation with a German:

And a little help if you want to make a date with a German friend:

Sprechen Sie Englisch?
(Do you speak English?)

Verstehen Sie mich?
(Do you understand me?)

Ich spreche nur wenig Deutsch
(I speak only a little German)

Bitte, sprechen Sie etwas langsamer
(Please, speak a little more slowly)

Ich bin Amerikaner
(I am an American)

Woher kommen Sie?
(Where are you from?)

Ich komme aus . . .
(I come from. . .)

Ich bin seit zehn Monaten in Deutschland
(I have been in Germany for ten months)

Mein Name ist . . . (My name is . . .)

Haben Sie (hast Du) heute nachmittag/abend schon etwas vor?
(Have you planned anything for this afternoon/evening?)

Haben Sie (hast Du) morgen abend Zeit?
(Are you free tomorrow night?)

Darf ich Sie/dich zu einer Tasse Kaffee/zu einem Glas Wein/zu einem Drink/zum Essen einladen?
(May I invite you for a cup of coffee/for a glass of wine/for a drink/for dinner?)

Wollen wir heute abend ins Kino/Tanzen gehen?
(Shall we go to the movies/dancing tonight?)

Ja, gern. (Yes, I'd like to)

Nein, tut mir leid, ich habe schon etwas vor.
(No, I'm sorry, I've already got something to do)

Wie wär's denn morgen?
(What about tomorrow?)

Ja, das paßt mir gut.
(Yes, that would suit me well)

Ich hole Sie/dich um . . . Uhr ab
(I will come to meet you at . . . o'clock)

Asking One's Way

Let's assume you have just arrived in a German town. You wish to look up your father's elderly sister who still lives in the same house from which your father emigrated to the States 30 years ago. You know the name of the street, but unfortunately you do not have a map of the town *(Stadtplan)* with you. How can you ask your way in German?

✳

Shortly after reaching the town, you see two housewives chatting on a street corner. You stop, roll down your window and ask, *"Entschuldigen Sie bitte, können Sie mir wohl sagen, wie ich zur Neustädter Straße komme?"* (Excuse me please, could yo tell me how to get to the Neustädter Straße?)

"Neustädter Straße", the one repeats. She turns around and stretches out her arm in the direction in which your car is heading. *"Immer geradeaus, junger Mann, ein ganzes Stück, und dann fragen Sie noch mal!"* (Always straight ahead, young man, for quite a while, and then ask once more!)

"Danke sehr" (thank you), you say. She answer, *"Bitte sehr!"* (You're welcome).

After "a while", you come to a large crossing, where a policemen directs the traffic. As he is in a big hurry, you ask him very shortly, *"Zur Neustädter Straße, wie muß ich da fahren, bitte?"* (To Neustädter Straße, where do I go, please?)

"Hier rechts", he answers, nodding to the right, *"und dann die zweite Querstraße links!"* (To the right here, and then take the second crossroad to the left.)

Again you do not forget your *"Danke schön"* and head for the right.

Alas, at the second crossing, there are two roads leading to the left! None of them is called "Neustädter Straße". Tentatively, you drive down the bigger one of the two until you see an old man. Again rolling down your window, you stop and ask, *"Verzeihung, geht es hier zur Neustädter Straße?"* (Excuse me, is this the right way to Neustädter Straße?)

The man nods, *"Ja, da sind Sie richtig, dies ist die Verlängerung von der Neustädter Straße. Fahren Sie noch ein Stück weiter, dann kommt eine große Rechtskurve, und dann sind Sie auf der Neustädter Straße!"* (Yes, you are on the right way, this is the extension of Neustädter Straße. Drive a little further, then there is a big curve to the right, and then you are on Neustädter Straße). Relieved, you say *"Vielen Dank"*, and he answers, *"Nichts zu danken!"* (Don't mention it).

And two minutes later you stand before your father's house.

P. S. Foreigners often are confused by the fact that in the larger German towns several sections of one and the same street bear different names. After passing an intersection you may find that "Neustädter Straße" suddenly is called "Parkallee", and several kilometers farther, what is apparently the same street now bears the name of "Bergstraße". On long roads, this may happen four or five or six times.

This came about because in centuries of expansion cities often have incorporated a number of formerly independent villages and towns, whose old street names were retained.

Talking About the Weather

Der Schauer = shower

Der Regen = rain

Bedeckter Himmel = overcast sky

Wolkig = cloudy

Das Gewitter = thunderstorm

Das Wetter wird besser = the weather is going to be better

Es wird schön = it is going to be nice

Die Sonne kommt durch = the sun is coming through

Die Wolken reißen auf = the clouds are breaking up

Der Wind läßt nach = the wind is letting up

Schönes/gutes/schlechtes Wetter = fine/good/bad weather

Es ist warm/heiß = it is warm/hot

Es ist kühl/kalt = it is chilly/cold

Es schneit = it snows

Es ist windig = it is windy

Es stürmt = it storms

Nebel = fog

Sprühregen = drizzle

Gewitter = thunderstorm

Blitz/Donner = lightning/thunder

ein klarer Tag = a clear day

Hochdruckgebiet = high-pressure area

Tiefdruckgebiet = low-pressure area

Frische Luft

It seems as if the Germans are especially "air-conscious". More than other people, they speak about the qualities of the air — be it *gute Luft, frische Luft, milde Luft, kalte Luft, feuchte Luft* or whatever.

A *Luftkurort* is a health resort where the air is considered particularly good — located in a forest, for instance.

Germans also speak of a "change of air" *(Luftveränderung)* if they mean that a change of climate will do their health good.

All this, of course, doesn't keep them from having an absolute horror of drafts. Even on the hottest summer day when you are dying to feel a breeze (the Germans, too — but only outdoors!) someone will close either a window or a door because *es zieht* (there's a draft) and you'll catch a cold.

At the Beauty Shop/Barber Shop — Beim Friseur

Have you yet had the fun of having your hair done at a German beauty parlor? If the answer is no, perhaps it is because you feel your "fractured" German might result in a Fiji-Island hairdo. This short vocabulary will help you.

First the basics:

frisieren — to dress the hair
die Frisur — hairdo
der Friseur — barber, barber shop, hair dresser
der Friseursalon — beauty shop
die Friseuse — beauty operator

When you enter the beauty shop, a young lady asks you *"Bitte sehr?"* (What can I do for you?)

"Waschen und legen, bitte!" (shampoo and set, please), you answer.

"Können Sie wohl zehn Minuten warten?" (Could you wait for about 10 minutes?) she asks. *"Ja, ich warte"* (yes, I'll wait), you say. *"Bitte, nehmen Sie Platz"* (please have a seat), she says and helps you take off your coat.

At last the waiting period is over. An operator seats you at a sink. She wraps a plastic cape around your shoulders, then may hand you a small cloth. This is for your eyes, because in Germany often one's hair is still washed with the forehead pointed down toward the sink. The operator will want to know what kind of shampoo to use. Just tell her, *"Ich habe fettiges (trockenes) Haar."* (I have oily (dry) hair.)

"Wie soll ich Ihr Haar frisieren?" (How shall I set your hair?) she asks. Here are a few expressions that may help you:

please cut it	*bitte schneiden*
on the sides	*an den Seiten*
in back	*hinten*
the bangs	*der Pony* (short "o")
longer in back	*hinten länger*
full on the sides	*die Seiten voll*
curly	*kraus*
straight	*glatt*
the permanent	*die Dauerwelle*
the set	*die Wasserwelle, das Einlegen*
blow dry	*fönen*

to dye, to tint	*färben, tönen*
hair styling gel	*das Haar-Gel*
hair spray	*das Haarspray*
wave set	*der Haarfestiger*
rollers	*Lockenwickler*
hair dryer	*die Trockenhaube*
tease	*toupieren*

Finally comes the time to pay for your new creation. Cutting, wave set, hair spray and so forth will be considered extras and added to the basic price for washing and setting. Don't forget to give a tip to the girl who did your hair. The owner of the salon is never tipped.

★

And here are a few expressions especially for the benefit of our male readers if they wish to have their hair cut in a German barber shop:

normal haircut, tapered back	*Fasson*
square back	*Rundschnitt*
trim the ends	*Spitzen abschneiden*
trim	*ausputzen*
shortened on top	*oben etwas kürzer*

What Time Is It?

How do you ask for the time? You can ask *"Wie spät ist es?"* or *"Wieviel Uhr ist es?"*

Here are some examples of telling time in German:

9:30 = *halb zehn*

7:45 = *viertel vor acht* or: *dreiviertel acht*

11:05 = *fünf nach elf*

3:50 = *zehn vor vier*

8:15 = *viertel nach acht* or: *ein Viertel neun*

10 a. m. = *zehn Uhr morgens*

10 p. m. = *zehn Uhr abends*

This is the colloquial usage. In official language, on the radio, or wherever it is important to avoid misunderstandings, one uses the figures 13 *(dreizehn)* to 24 *(vierundzwanzig)* for the afternoon hours (military time). For 8:15 p. m., the radio announcer will say *"Es ist jetzt zwanzig Uhr fünfzehn"*. For five minutes past midnight, he would say *"Null Uhr fünf"*, literally: zero hour five.

ein Viertel vor drei
or: dreiviertel drei
or: zwei (vierzehn) Uhr fünfundvierzig

For longer periods: The phrase "a week from today" can be expressed either as *"heute in einer Woche"* or *"heute in acht Tagen"*. In two weeks is *"in 14 Tagen"* or *"in zwei Wochen."*

Reading and Writing German Figures

The way German figures are written often is confusing for newcomers to Germany. To Americans, the German numeral "one" may look like an American "seven" and the "seven" has a slight resemblance to a backward capital "F", as it has its stem crossed.

Another difference when reading German figures: the period separates billions, millions, thousands and hundreds, while the comma sets off the decimal fraction.

American usage: US $ 10,000.50
German usage: DM 10.000,50

When the numbers get bigger than a million the vocabulary gets confusing: an American million equals a German one but an American billion (= *Milliarde* in German) is 1,000 times smaller than a German *Billion* (= American trillion).

Day Before Month

Dates, too, are written differently: first the day, then the month, and finally the year, with no comma in-between: *20. November 1989 = 20. 11. 1989* (beware of this trap when filling in German forms!)

Don't Let the Dialects Throw You!

Many an American who came to Germany with what he thought was a good command of German got the shock of his life once a German started to speak to him. Not understanding a word, he wondered what kind of language he had actually learned at school. Maybe he came to a small town in Bavaria, Swabia, the Palatinate, or Hesse. In those southern and central parts of Germany, local dialects are sometimes especially difficult to understand for foreigners — even for North Germans. Plattdeutsch, still spoken in rural areas of Lower Saxony, Westphalia and Schleswig-Holstein and in the ports, is closer to English but chances are it throws the stranger just as well.

Everyone Understands High German

The German spoken in Hannover is generally considered to be the best High-German. Educated people all over the country are able to speak High-German (although often with a shade of the local dialect), and practically everybody can understand it. And slowly, the foreigner will learn to understand the dialect, too. No reason for frustration!

A Metzger Is a Fleischer

Although West Germany is a small country, there are many differences between regions — not only in the customs but also in the use of the language. For instance:

In Hamburg, a butcher is called *Schlachter*, in Berlin *Schlächter*, but in southern and western Germany the same profession is known as *Metzger*, in central Germany as *Fleischer* and in the Southeast as *Fleischhacker* or sometimes as *Selcher*.

Similarly, a plumber or tinsmith is called *Klempner* in most areas but in the south, *Spengler*.

The best example for differences in food names is the roll: *Brötchen* is the most generally accepted term, but you also find *Semmel* or *Weck* (South Germany), *Schrippe* (Berlin), or *Rundstück* (Hamburg).

Berlin, Germany

"We went to Munich, Germany, and then to Brussels, Belgium, and on to Madrid, Spain," an American tourist would say in describing his European travels; from the huge U. S. A. he is used to adding the state to the city name. Not so the European. Normally, he would not add the countries' name in this case. Nor would a German add the federal state's name (Rheinland-Pfalz, Hesse, Bavaria) to the city, as hardly any misunderstandings are possible. "Ich komme aus Köln und will nach Mannheim," he would just say.

The House Floor Confusion

It's easy to mix up the house floors in Germany. What Americans call the first floor the Germans call the *Parterre* or *Erdgeschoss*. Second floor would be *I. Stock* or *I. Etage* in German, third floor *II. Stock*, etc.

Old, Old Towns

Germany still is a picture book of history — at least for those who can read it. Take the names of the towns, for instance: if you know a little bit about their origin, you will look at the places with different eyes. Many town names go back to Roman and Germanic or Celtic times.

A lot of towns in the South and West of Germany originated at the time when the Romans occupied these areas, viz. roughly 2,000 to 1,500 years ago. Examples are Augsburg, Cologne, Regensburg, Wiesbaden, Kassel, Koblenz, Pforzheim.

A nearby castle (Burg) often gave the town its name (Hamburg, Rothenburg). Other frequent elements in German place names include Bach, Bad, Berg, Feld, Fels, Furt, Hafen or Haven, Heim, Hof, Kirche, Mühle, Stein, Tal, Wald, etc.

Something on Proverbs

**Germans and Americans have many proverbs in common, although the pictures
they use are not always the same. It is interesting to compare some:**

German

*Ein Spatz in der Hand ist besser als die
Taube auf dem Dach.*
(A sparrow in the hand is better than a
dove on the roof)

*Wer andern eine Grube gräbt, fällt selbst
hinein.*
(He who digs a trap for others will fall into
it himself)

Wo gehobelt wird, fallen Späne.
(Where one planes, there will be shavings)

Vom Regen in die Traufe.
(From the rain into the gutter)

*Es wird nichts so heiß gegessen wie es ge-
kocht wird.*
(Nothing is eaten as hot as it is cooked)

*Wenn man den Wolf nennt, kommt er
gerennt.*
(If you name the wolf he comes running)

Aus der Mücke einen Elefanten machen.
(To make an elephant out of a mosquito)

American

A bird in the hand is worth two in the
bush.

He that mischief hatcheth, mischief cat-
cheth.

You cannot make an omelette without
breaking eggs.

From the frying pan into the fire.

Things are not as black they look.

Speak of the devil, and he is sure to appear.

To make a mountain out of a molehill.

"Der Apfel fällt nicht weit vom Stamm" —
a chip off the old block.

Shopping in Germany

For foreigners speaking little German and who are unfamiliar with German customs, shopping is easier in the large department stores and supermarkets. They look pretty much the same all over the Western world, and you can browse to your heart's content practically without having to speak to a salesperson.

It's different in the smaller shops and boutiques, but you shouldn't avoid them for fear of having to speak because you might miss an opportunity to get in touch with the "real Germany" that you had wanted to meet ever since coming over. Besides, many salespersons do speak a little English.

A Few Tips

It's customary to say *"Guten Tag"* when entering a small shop and *"Auf Wiedersehen"* when leaving. When you are approached by a salesperson and you're not ready to buy something yet, say *"ich möchte mich nur umsehen"* (just browsing). For "I'll have to think it over" you might say *"Ich muß es mir nochmal überlegen"*. Footwear and clothing you should always try on *(anprobieren)* as not only the sizes vary but also the cuts, and there are additional variations between products from various countries — France, Italy, Greece, Spain, East European or Far East countries. The exchange of items bought is called *Umtausch*.

Look for *Sonderangebot* and *Sonderpreis* (reduced prices) but beware of the large price signs that show the word *ab* before the price: *"Hemden ab 10,--"*. This means "and up", and usually there will be just a very few shirts at 10,-- available and all the others are "and up". Therefore, always read the individual price tag, too.

For paying, look for the sign *Kasse*.

Souvenir items you should buy in big German stores, not at the souvenir stands where the quality and selection usually is not so good and the prices are higher.

German supermarkets operate pretty much the same as those elsewhere, except that the products are named differently

Outdoor markets enjoy great popularity in Germany, in small towns as well as in big cities.

(c) ZEFA-Teasy

The variety of German sausage specialties is immense: Altogether, there are more than 1,500 different kinds.

(c) ZEFA-Teasy

Shopping (continued)

and the weights are metric. Meat is cut differently, and this, we're afraid, is something that you can only learn by trying what is offered here.

Even in the largest supermarkets there will normally be no "bagger" to pack your groceries and carry them out to your car. Wages are just too high in Germany for such "luxury", so you'll have to be your own bagger. In many places you can use the same cart with which you took the merchandise to the cashier to transport them to the parking lot. Generally plastic — not brown paper — bags are available but they often cost a bit extra (usually ten Pfennigs).

Credit Cards, Charge Accounts

Germans pay in cash or, in the case of larger sums, with the popular "euro-cheque" (see page 35). Many shops and restaurants accept the major international credit cards, but on the whole credit cards are not used very much in Germany. Europeans are always struck by the bundles of credit cards some Americans are carrying around.

Thrift Mentality

Foreigners sometimes wonder how the average German wage-earner makes ends meet in view of the high prices in Germany. The answer lies in a certain "thrift mentality".

Most Germans shop very carefully, always comparing prices and taking advantage of special offers or sales. When buying more expensive items they usually look for high, durable quality.

Installment buying is well know here, too, particularly for cars and furniture. Some department stores offer charge accounts.

No State Taxes

When you see a price tag in a German store you can be sure that it shows the final price, all taxes included. There are no special state taxes or sales taxes that might be added.

Most small shops have given way to supermarkets and department stores. Those which remained often stick out for specialities, high quality, and personalized service.

Think Metric

Ordering small quantities of cold cuts is quite common in Germany.

A kilometer is a little more than half a mile, 10 kilometers are 6 miles.

Thirty degrees Celsius mean a hot day.

Overcome the Measuring Barrier!

There is much talk of the language barrier separating Americans from their European surroundings. What many forget is another barrier, just as frustrating, but much easier to overcome — the measuring barrier.

You're in the middle of Frau Schmidt's favorite cookie recipe, and are stopped short by the notation "150 grams flour".

A German friend tells you in horror that it was 38 degrees during his Italian vacation and you don't know whether he sweltered or froze.

Your car needs 10 gallons of gas and the attendant asks, "How many liters, please?"

While the U. S. is gradually switching over to the metric system, Americans coming to Europe are plunged into a metric world.

Think Metric!

Living in Europe is a lot simpler for the American who "thinks metric" from the start. He can go into any store and order with authority, without depending on some helpful sales clerk or fellow buyer who will convert for him.

If you start out with two basic facts, you'll do fine with the metric system from the beginning. First, remember that measurements are based on 100, not all kinds of

numbers like 16 ounces to a pound, or 5, 280 feet in a mile. Second, the prefix "centi" means hundredth; "kilo" means thousand.

Thus, a meter has 100 centimeters; a kilometer has 1,000 meters. Similarly, a kilogram has 1,000 grams, a liter 100 centiliters, and so on.

As we said, it's much better to start thinking metrically instead of always converting from American measurements, but one has to start, of course, from comparisons:

A meter is about 39 inches;
a kilogram, or kilo, is 2.2 pounds;
a liter is 2.113 pints;
a kilometer is 5/8 of a mile.

For practical purposes you don't usually have to be so exact. Supposing you want to buy some yardage for a dress. Since a meter is slightly more than a yard, you know you'll have some left over if you order four meters when the pattern calls for four yards.

Or you need 10 gallons of gas. Since there are about four liters in a gallon, you'll buy 40 liters.

Measuring Barrier (continued)

Shopping for food, you have another help, because many Germans still commonly measure by the *Pfund*, or pound. A *Pfund* is a half kilo, or 500 grams. This makes it just slightly more than the U. S. pound (454 grams).

Ein Achtel Wurst

A delight to the housewife with a small family is the German custom of selling foods in very small quantities. And if you'd like to serve a large variety of cheese and sausages, you can order them by units of one or several hundred grams. Prices, however, are by kilos (1,000 grams).

Milk, cream, wine and other liquids are measured by the liter — a little over a quart.

When it comes to recipes, things are not so easy. Germans are not used to measuring cups and spoons, but use scales instead. This is a much more exact system, which eliminates such American complications as sifting flour before measuring it. A hundred grams of flour, after all, weigh 100 grams, sifted or not.

You won't be far off, however, if you estimate a cup of sugar as 200 grams; a cup of flour, 150 grams; a teaspoonful, 5 grams, a tablespoonful, 12 grams.

Shopping for clothes is probably the least of your problems. If the purchase is for you, the salesperson can easily estimate your size. Many large department stores have conversion tables of American and German sizes, and most salespeople who commonly wait on Americans know these by heart.

The conversion table at the end of this booklet will help you with dresses, shoes, shirts, etc. Stocking sizes in Germany are the same as in America.

But we still haven't found out if our German friend sweltered or froze during his Italian vacation. Well, to begin with, 32 degrees Fahrenheit, or freezing, is 0 degrees Celsius. To figure out all other temperatures, simply take the Celsius reading, multiply by 9, divide by 5 and add 32. So, now do you know?

Carlotta Anderson

Drogerie Is Not Drugstore

A German *Drogerie* is not quite the same as an American drugstore. A *Drogerie* will sell toiletries, household cleansers, babyfood, camera supplies, wallpaper, seeds, paints, etc. but it does not deal in prescription medicine, nor does it offer food or drinks.

Parfümerie

A *Parfümerie* sells cosmetics, perfumes, soaps, etc.

Apotheke

An *Apotheke* (pharmacy) sells medicine with and without prescriptions, and also some toilet articles.

Reformhaus

A *Reformhaus* is comparable with an American Health or Natural Food Store. It sells special foods, teas and vitamins. Many a *Reformhaus* has turned into a goldmine with the health food boom that has swept Germany in recent years.

Buying Clothes and Shoes

"Bitte sehr?" the sales girl *(die Verkäuferin)* asks. *"Werden Sie schon bedient?"* (Are you being helped?)
"Ich möchte. . . Ich hätte gern. . . (I'd like) — ein Kleid (dress), eine Bluse (blouse), einen Rock (skirt), ein Kostüm (suit), or einen Mantel (coat)." A pullover is also called *"Pullover"* in German, but with the stress on the second syllable, or *"Pulli".*

"Welche Größe haben Sie?" (what size do you wear?) is the next question. Know the German sizes? To get the German sizes, add 8 to the U. S. sizes for blouses, 28 to those for skirts, dresses and coats, and 31 to those for shoes. For example, if you wear a size 14 dress in the States, you'll take a German size 42. *"Wollen Sie es anprobieren?"* (Do you wish to try it on?)

"Ich möchte ein Paar schwarze Schuhe, Größe 43, bitte" (I want a pair of black shoes, size 12, please). Some more terms that you might need: *"zu eng"* — too narrow; *"zu weit"* — too wide; *"zu spitz"* — too pointed; *"zu breit"* — too broad. (For the ladies: high heels are *"hohe Absätze"* in German, medium heels — *"halbhohe Absätze"*, flat heels — *"flache Absätze"*)

Shops Close Early

Americans intending to shop in German stores are often confused and irritated by the early hours at which German shops close their doors. The shop owners are obliged to do so on account of a Federal law which was intended to protect the interests of small shopkeepers and shop personnel.

Criticism against this law is growing, however, and many Germans, especially working housewives, hope that it will be modified. Plans are under way to allow later closing hours for at least one evening per week, probably on Thursdays.

Closing Times Prescribed

Presently, all shops, with some exceptions, are obliged by law to close Monday through Friday from 6:30 p.m. until 7 a.m. the following day and at 2 p.m. Saturday.

On every first Saturday in the month and on the four Saturdays before Christmas shops can be kept open until 6 p.m. Within these limits, shop owners can fix their individual opening and closing hours. In vil-

Nothing doing after 6.30 p.m.

lages and small towns, as well as in the suburbs of bigger cities, many stores close for an hour or so around noontime.

Exceptions

Stands selling fruit, candy, newspapers and similar articles at railway stations and airports can be kept open outside the normal closing hours.

Outside the hours fixed for all other shops, they are supposed to sell only to customers using the trains or planes, but this law is often ignored. Other exceptions from the rule were introduced for tourist spots during the season, when shops may be open all day on Saturday and also on Sunday afternoons.

The law allows certain shops to open also on Sundays. The hours differ in the various states. Milk shops may be open on Sunday mornings; flower shops around noon; and bakery shops, selling their own cakes, in the early afternoon. Newspapers can be sold from 11 a.m. until 1 p.m. (sometimes also in the morning) on Sundays and from 6 a.m. until 7 p.m. every weekday.

Sales and Markets

Everyone Likes A Bargain

German shops have their big clearance sales, called *Winter-* or *Sommerschlußverkauf* or *Ausverkauf*, two weeks in winter and two weeks in summer (starting officially on the last Monday in January and the last Monday in July). Many shops, however, begin their *Ausverkauf* much earlier, offering certain items at reduced prices (*reduziert* or *Sonderangebot*) immediately before or after Christmas and in the early summer.

"Handeln"

Most people in Germany are not used to bargaining (*"handeln"*) and even regard it as demeaning. It is certainly not the usual way of doing business here, but in some areas it has become more acceptable. It depends very much on the item you wish to buy. Nobody will be offended if you try your bargaining skills at a flea market or when buying a second-hand car.

The Outdoor Markets

Regularly on market days (once or twice a week), summer and winter, outdoor markets are held all over Germany, in small towns as well as in big cities. Everywhere on the market places one can see the heavily laden counters of eggs, salami and cheese, the tables piled high with fruit and vegetables, the stands selling fish and meat, flowers and household utensils, inexpensive books and clothes. There is always a bustling, lively atmosphere about these markets, with the dealers crying their wares, enticing the swarming buyers to buy from their goods and not that of their neighbor.

The *Markt* in modern Europe is to be seen today practically as it was many centuries ago. So if it's a bargain you want and a little bit of "Old Europe", then the market place is a must.

Two of three German housewives like to buy at the street market if they have the opportunity. Local authorities supervise these markets and see to it that the sanitary regulations are observed.

Flea markets (*Flohmarkt* or *Trödelmarkt*) are also very popular all over Germany.

But the popular American institution of "garage sales" is hardly known over here.

Folk Festivals, Holiday Customs, Leisure Time Pursuits

Meet Merry People

A great number of folk festivals take place in Germany every year. Preserved from olden days, when the individual regions of the country still had little contact with the outside world, festivals developed according to the particular customs of the area.

These folk festivals always meet with great interest not only on the part of the German population but also on the part of foreign visitors.

World-famous, of course, is the Munich Oktoberfest. Other more intimate events, however, are no less attractive. Some of these include the "Shepherds' Dance" in Rothenburg ob der Tauber, the *"Kinderzeche"* in Dinkelsbühl, the "Fishermen's Jousting" in Ulm, the "Goat Auction" in Deidesheim and the "Shepherds' Run" in Markgröningen and Urach.

In the late summer and in autumn, wine festivals are celebrated in all wine growing regions: on the Rhine, in the Palatinate, on the Moselle, Nahe, Ruwer and Saar rivers, in the Eifel area, along the "Mountain Road" between Heidelberg and Darmstadt, in Baden, Württemberg, at Lake Constance and in Franconia. The first wine festivals take place as early as June, but the season really begins in September, with the wine harvesting season.

The largest German wine festival, which dates back to the year 1442, is held annually in Bad Dürkheim, between Mannheim and Kaiserslautern. The festival is called *"Wurstmarkt"* (Sausage Fair) and attracts more than 500,000 visitors.

A local poet put it this way: "The Sausage Fair is a festival where you meet lots of friends you have never seen before in all your life."

Other big wine festivals are in Koblenz, Heppenheim, Mainz, Rüdesheim, Assmanshausen, Bacharach, Trier and Bingen. In Neustadt in the Palatinate "Wine Queens" are chosen and the new wine is given its name.

Oktoberfest in September

Although called *Oktoberfest*, most of this gigantic affair takes place during the latter part of September. It ends early in October. It really is the Bavarian National Festival and as such the emphasis is on drinking Bavarian beer, not wine. Incredible quantities of *Wiesenbier,* which is especially strong, are downed every year at the *Oktoberfest,* together with many tons of pork sausages, roasted chickens and oxen on the spit. About seven million visitors attend the festival each year.

The big "fest" begins with the entrance of the proprietors of the beer halls on the Theresienwiese (or simply: *Wies'n*) and the tapping of the first cask by the Lord Mayor. On the following day there is the great *Trachtenfest* parade, with thousands of participants in folk costumes, with bands, floats and decorated beer wagons drawn by the famous brewery horses. The parade winds through Munich's downtown streets and ends on the festival grounds, the *Wies'n.*

Harvest Thanksgiving

Harvest Thanksgiving is celebrated in numerous ways all over rural Germany. The churches hold special services. Harvest wreaths of wheat and colorful ribbons are a traditional feature. It is not a legal holiday in Germany, however, and not celebrated in the family with such traditional foods as cranberry sauce and pumpkin pie.

In some areas, these festivities fall together with *Allerweltskirchweih* on the third Sunday in October.

Kirchweih

Kirchweih — also called *Kirmes, Kirchtag, Kerb, Kilbe,* or simply *Jahrmarkt* — is an annual event usually observed in small

Karneval, Fasching — The Crazy Time

An American coming directly from New York to Mainz or Cologne on Rose Monday might easily believe that the Germans had suddenly gone crazy. In the streets he would see crowds of laughing, singing people, often dancing or swaying arm in arm in crazy costumes and masks. Those days before Ash Wednesday, usually in

(continued on page 112)

communities. It has its historical roots in the church consecration festivities. An annual market often was part of the festival, and gradually amusement fairs developed as a standing feature of the *Kirchweih*, with merry-go-rounds, shooting galleries, and all kinds of booths and stands.

Karneval, Fasching — The Crazy Time (continued)

February, are the climax of the carnival season. *Karneval* is most enthusiastically celebrated in those parts of Germany where there is a Catholic majority, particularly in the South and in the Rhineland.

Today it may seem as if carnival is nothing more than an outburst of gaiety and enjoyment of life before Lent begins. But actually in olden times there was a different meaning behind all this.

The custom springs from pre-Christian roots, having developed from superstitious fears at the change of the seasons, when demons who might win power over man had to be exorcized by noise, lights and conjurings. It was believed that men dressed up as demons and witches, animals or spirits were better able to take up the battle with supernatural powers, to help the spring season overcome the demons of winter. In time the Church condoned the ancient pagan practices by regarding them as a legitimate period of healthy release of merriment before Lent.

Cologne, Mainz and Munich are regarded as the three major "carnival cities" of Germany, and each of the three claims its own style of playing the fool under the scepter of Prince Carnival.

The Rhineland's Karneval

Cologne prides itself on the fact that its best carnival talent comes from the narrow streets and alleys of the oldest parts of the city. In January and February, carnival societies hold dozens of *Sitzungen* which include plenty of drinking, singing, *schunkeln* (swaying arm in arm) and laughing. Odd folk characters tell their funny stories in broad dialect and sing their songs. In the middle of January, "Prince Carnival" is proclaimed in a merry ceremony in which the mayor invests the elected "Prince" with sovereignty over the city. Cologne has no "Princess Carnival" like other cities but, instead, the *Kölnischer Bauer* (the Peasant of Cologne) and the *Kölnische Jungfrau* (the Virgin of Cologne).

The latter is always a man — a relic of the old times when the fair sex was excluded from the carnival altogether. Women were admitted on only one day. From this tradition remains the custom that the Thursday of the week before Ash Wednesday is reserved for *Weiberfastnacht* (Women's Carnival). On this day, the women reign over the cities of the Rhineland, including the capital of the Federal Republic, Bonn, with its government agencies and ministries.

Fancydress Balls, Parades

This is the beginning of the carnival proper. On Friday and Saturday the big masquerades and fancy-dress balls take place. On Sunday afternoon in Cologne, the various quarters of the city and the schools have their special carnival street parades, which sometimes are even more original than the "official" parade on Rose Monday, which is considered the ultimate climax of Karneval. The official parade is four to five miles long. In slow procession, it winds through the city, with huge floats, horses, funny groups of jesters wearing grotesque or comical masks, and marching bands of the Fools Guilds in their traditional picturesque uniforms. The city is turned upside down, and normal business is practically at a standstill.

Fassenacht in Mainz

Carnival in the other Rhineland cities follows very much the same pattern, with local variations. Mainz *Fassenacht* honors a tradition of political satire dating back to the times of the French revolutionary wars. The carnival *Sitzungen* in Mainz are especially popular all over Germany because they have been shown on nationwide TV for many years. Also, the Mainzers have an unusual number of very picturesque "Guards" in their big Rose Monday parade, wearing historical uniforms.

Munich Fasching

Munich, where carnival is called *Fasching*, boasts a traditional carnival spirit born of more southern, more light hearted regions. By way of Vienna, the splendor of the Venetian carnival has had an influence on the innumerable balls that take place at this time of the year.

A very old feature of Munich's fasching is the "Dance of the Coopers" which is presented only every seven years in the streets of the city. It originated in the Middle Ages, after the plague had swept the country. The coopers were the first courageous ones to go out into the streets and with all kinds of dances and merry-making tried to get people out of their houses again.

Carnival is not limited to the big cities alone; throughout Bavaria and the Rhineland, many small towns, too, compete with each other in arranging carnival processions and setting up princes of their own.

Swabian Fasnet

Something rather special is carnival in Swabia, where it is called *Fasnet*. Traces of ancient Germanic cult practices are to be found much more clearly here than in other regions.

Members of the Fools Guilds, masked grotesquely, sway and weave through the streets in the traditional *Narrensprung*, a remnant of the ancient pre-Christian priests' ritual. There is *Federhannes*, with a feathered headdress, and *Schantele*, whose mask depicts half sadness, half joy and who hops along in rhythm to the music with his walking stick and umbrella. Most striking, though, are the *Gschell-Narren* who carry 40 pound sets of bells around their necks. Their masks show huge, gaping mouths with teeth, and the bells make a deafening noise.

These customs are best preserved in Rottweil, a little town on the Neckar river, but many other towns and villages in the region observe carnival time in very much the same fashion.

But wherever it may be — at midnight Tuesday, when Lent begins, the days of exuberant joyfulness find a sudden, almost dramatic end.

No "Grabbing for Checks"

A word of advice in case you attend a folk-festival for the first time: generally, there is little "treating." Each orders and pays for his own beer and food. If a German should offer to buy you a beer, accept with thanks, then later on reciprocate. However, there is no check grabbing.

Richtfest

A wreath of pine branches decorated with colored streamers shows that the completion of the roof framework has been celebrated.

Wherever a new building is erected in Germany, a special celebration, the *Richtfest*, is held when the roof's framework is raised. A wreath of pine branches, decorated with colored streamers, is placed on top of the unfinished roof or on top of a crane. In many places a decorated bush, looking almost like a Christmas tree, takes the place of the wreath.

Then the foreman *(Polier)* climbs up and delivers a speech in poetry to the construction workers, the architect, the home owners and their guests, expressing joy over the completed work and asking God's blessing on the house. He drinks a glass of wine and, to bring good luck, smashes the glass on the structure.

Afterwards, all assemble in a half-completed room of the new house or in a tavern for more drinking and hearty eating, plus more speeches. The tab for the day is picked up by the builder *(Bauherr)*.

Journeymen Carpenters

The picturesque black costume of the journeymen carpenters is an old tradition. They wear bell-bottomed corduroy pants, matching vest and jacket with mother-of-pearl buttons and a floppy, wide-brimmed hat, a gold earring worn in the left ear, and a gnarled walking stick.

If you are lucky, you may see groups of these picturesque characters along the highway as they are traveling the countryside. They work with various master craftsmen for three years and one day. Nowhere are they allowed to stay longer than two months.

Formerly, this used to be the custom for journeymen of all crafts, but today only an estimated 150 to 200, all belonging to the construction trade, are going *"auf die Walz"* (the journey, hence the name journeyman).

Schützenfest

More than a million marksmen are organized in West Germany's 12,800 *Schützenvereine* (marksmen's associations). Their traditional festivals are very popular in many towns and villages, particularly in the states of Lower Saxony, Bavaria, and North Rhine Westphalia. They are a combination of marksmanship competitions, including the selection of a *Schützenkönig* or king, and general fair activities.

"Laternegehen" and "Schultüten"

"Sonne, Mond und Sterne". . .

During the first weeks of fall, when the evenings are getting longer, you can sometimes see groups of children in the dark carrying candle-lit bright paper lanterns through the streets as they sing of the sun, moon and stars. Mostly they just walk along with mother, but some towns arrange big lantern parades.

This is a fall custom primarily in Northern Germany, while the St. Martin's lantern parades in November take place in the predominantly Catholic West and South of the country.

Another nice custom connected with children:

On the first day of school, parents give their little kids huge, colorful cardboard cones filled with sweets or small toys. This is to help sweeten a little their first day away from home.

(For more details on German holidays and the customs connected with them, see our booklet "German Holidays and Folk Customs".)

The first day of school.

Traditional Costumes and Houses

Hessian Folk Costumes

Only if you are very lucky, and only in rural areas of Germany (particularly in Hesse, Bavaria, and the Black Forest), can you sometimes still see people wearing the old folk costumes. Today, they wear them only on church holidays, or for weddings and similar occasions.

Chimney Sweep

Another picturesque remnant from olden times is the hat and black outfit worn by German chimney sweeps (Schornsteinfeger or Kaminkehrer).
Most Germans believe meeting a chimney sweep or even touching him brings them good luck.

Traditional Farm Houses

If you have an opportunity to do some traveling in Germany, you will notice that the older farm houses differ greatly from one region to the other. This house is typical of Hesse/Frankonia.

Wedding Customs

How To Congratulate

"Polterabend", on the eve of the wedding, is a popular custom in Germany. Friends of the couple go to the bride's house and smash old pottery at the door or under her window. It's an old superstition that the loud noise helps to avert bad luck. To assure future married bliss, the bride is expected to sweep up the broken pieces all by herself.

Some American customs, such as the big wedding cake, the throwing of confetti or rice, or bridal showers are not part of the German tradition. Presents are delivered on Polterabend or on the wedding day itself. — In Germany, the civil marriage at the local "Standesamt" (registrar's office) is obligatory. A church wedding follows the civil marriage.

"Herzlichen Glückwunsch zum Geburtstag!" is the most accepted and popular form of congratulating a German on his birthday. The first two words, *Herzlichen Glückwunsch*, or the plural, *Herzliche Glückwünsche*, will fit on almost any occasion if you wish to congratulate someone in German, be it a birthday *(Geburtstag)*, a name-day *(Namenstag)*, an engagement *(Verlobung)*, a wedding *(Hochzeit)*, the birth or christening of a baby *(Geburt, Taufe)*, church confirmation or Communion, or an anniversary *(Jubiläum)*.

Germans make more fuss over the celebrating of their birthdays than do Americans. For example, instead of having a party given for them, they are expected to throw their own party and invite friends and family. This may be anything from just coffee and cake to an elaborate dinner party. Coming of age and "round" birthdays — 25, 30, 40, 50, etc. — are regarded as especially important — the older you get, the more so.

A little warning: Many Germans believe that congratulating ahead of time brings bad luck.

How To Congratulate (continued)

Greeting Cards

If you want to write your congratulations, you will probably use a greeting card. It is customary to add not only your name to the printed text but also some personal words, such as *"Mit allen guten Wünschen"* or *"Alles Gute für die Zukunft"* or whatever the occasion may suggest.

Popular wishes for Christmas and the New Year include *"Fröhliche Weihnachten und ein glückliches Neues Jahr!"* or perhaps *"Ein frohes Weihnachtsfest und viel Glück* (or *"alles Gute") zum Neuen Jahr!"* More formal would be: *"Mit den besten Wünschen zum Jahreswechsel!"*

In talking, most people wish each other *"Frohes Fest!"* on these occasions, also at Easter *(Ostern)* and Whitsuntide *(Pfingsten)*. But you can also wish *"Fröhliche Ostern!"* and *"Fröhliche Pfingsten!"*

Flowers and Presents

On receiving an engagement, wedding, or birth announcement, you should send a card with your congratulation with a bouquet of flowers.

Concerning presents, much depends on the relationship between you and the person to whom you want to give a present. This is the same as in the States. The American customs of bridal showers and baby showers are not known in Germany. Here, you send or bring flowers for the mother and/or a little present for the baby after he or she is born. Engagement presents are given or sent the day of the engagement. Wedding presents often are delivered at the house while the family is attending the church ceremony or — if you are invited to *Polterabend* — on the eve of the wedding. Likewise, christening presents are given when the family celebration takes place. If you are not invited to the christening but you are asked to "come and see the baby", bring flowers and a little present, too.

Flowers are also brought along when visiting sick people. And what do you wish a sick person? Say *"Weiterhin gute Besserung!"* or, more formal, *"Gute Genesung!"*

How to Answer

Last but not least you would perhaps like to know what to answer if a German congratulates you in German. Use any of the various *"danke"*-forms, like *Vielen Dank, Herzlichen Dank,* or *Vielen, herzlichen Dank,* adding perhaps *Nett, daß Sie gekommen sind* (nice of you to have come) or *Nett, daß Sie daran gedacht haben* (nice of you to think of it).

Scene from a carnival
"session" in Mainz,
one of the centers of
the Rhenish carnival.
(c) ZEFA-Kiedrowski

The Christmas Market in Frankfurt's Römer square. In the weeks before Christmas, you find these markets all over Germany.

(c) ZEFA-Hackenberg

Christmas Customs

The Advent Season

The German Christmas season starts with *Advent*, which is observed in many homes with an Advent wreath *(Adventskranz)*. Made of fir entwined with bright red ribbons and crowned with four candles, this wreath is either suspended from the chandelier in the living room or placed upon a table. However, the wreath form is increasingly abandoned and a less formal arrangement *(Gesteck)* of fir branches, fir cones, candles, etc. is used instead.

Each Sunday, one candle is lit for each week. On the last Sunday before Christmas all four candles have been lit and shed their mellow light — a prefiguration of the coming of Christ.

Many children are given Advent calendars which have 24 little doors. Beginning on December 1, the child opens a door each day to find a new picture. Sometimes he or she will also find a piece of candy.

German children are told that on the night of December 6, Saint Nicholas' Day, *"Nikolaus"* (St. Nick) with his long beard, bishop's miter and staff, will come on a donkey-drawn sled. Mostly his appearance is left up to the children's imagination, as he comes while they are sleeping. Instead of a stocking, many German children still place one of their shoes on the window sill or outside their door, and lo and behold, the next morning the shoes are filled with goodies.

Only in some southern regions does Saint Nicholas make a personal appearance in the evening of December 5; in this case, there is no *Weihnachtsmann* on Christmas Eve proper.

Christmas Markets

In the weeks before Christmas, Christmas Markets *(Weihnachtsmärkte)* are held in many towns — a custom which of late has gained in popularity. The *"Christkindlesmarkt"* in Nürnberg is particularly famous.

Real Candles

Although fir trees with electric candles appear on the streets, gardens, and balconies weeks before Christmas, in German homes the Christmas tree is usually not put up

A Tip for the Mailman

In Germany, too, it is customary to give Christmas presents or tips to people who helped you the year round, like the mailman, the newspaper boy, the cleaning woman, etc., but there is no hard and fast rule as to how much to give.

Christmas Customs (continued)

much earlier than on Christmas Eve itself.

Many Germans still prefer a tree with real candles.

To be on the safe side those who use real candles should keep some wet towels in the room — just in case. Real candles should be placed towards the tip of the limbs. The important thing is always to have someone present while the candles are burning.

The electric lights used in Germany are imitations of white or red candles, not colored or flickering lights as on many US Christmas trees.

Nativity Scenes

Some families have a Nativity Scene *(Krippe),* which is often handmade and a family heirloom.

Such manger scenes are also set up in many churches. In some places, "Krippenspiele" (Christmas plays) are still performed during the Christmas services, a custom dating from the Middle Ages.

Christmas Pastry

Christmas pastry has a long tradition. *Lebkuchen* and other sweet cookies of all kinds are still standard features of the family Christmas celebration in Germany. And so are *Christstollen* with raisins, nuts, and candied lemon and orange peels, as well as festive meals, often including roast goose, duck, or carp.

25th and 26th Are Holidays

Christmas Eve *(Heiliger Abend)* is the main event in Germany, and both the 25th and 26th of December are national holidays. On Christmas Eve, shops and offices close at 2 p.m.

Gifts are exchanged on Christmas Eve.

The counterpart of America's Santa Claus is the German *Weihnachtsmann* (literally Christmas man), in whom the figure of St. Nicholas has merged with older, demonic winter figures such as *Knecht Ruprecht* or *Krampus,* formerly believed to accompany St. Nicholas. In some South German regions, the *Christkind* (Christ Child, "Kris Kringle") is the mysterious gift-bringer.

More on Legal Holidays

The Germans observe their "Labor Day" *(Tag der Arbeit)* on the first of May. Traditional May Day celebrations with maypoles, etc. are still held in many German towns and villages on this day. As with most other holidays, however, many of the old customs are slowly disappearing.

Good Friday *(Karfreitag)* and Easter Monday *(Ostermontag)* are legal holidays in Germany, and so are Ascension Day *(Christi Himmelfahrt)* and the Monday after Whitsunday/Pentecost *(Pfingsten).*

June 17 is observed as the "Day of German Unity". It was established in the wake of the 1953 uprising of the popuation in the DDR (East Germany).

On the whole, Germans have more holidays than Americans, but no holiday with a fixed date is ever moved to a Friday or Monday.

Some religious holidays — *Heilige Drei Könige, Fronleichnam, Allerheiligen* — are legal holidays only in those states where the Catholic denomination is in the majority.

At a Dance

Dancing habits in Germany, as in the States, depend very much on the company and place. While there are practically no rules of etiquette left in discos or at young people's parties, they are still pretty much observed at more formal occasions. Here's how it's done the perfectly formal way:

A man who wants do dance with a girl approaches her table, bows slightly, and asks to dance with her *("Darf ich bitten?")*. After the dance, he accompanies his partner back to her seat, bows slightly once more and thanks her for the dance.

At more formal social events with dancing, a man is expected to dance not only with his wife or girl friend but also (at least once) with the wives of his friends and colleagues. In a round of people who know each other well, it is not uncommon anymore that women ask men to dance with them. The practice of *Abklatschen* (cutting in) is only known at very lively and relaxed German parties.

The formal way of asking for a dance. Dances are in series of two or three. You normally dance all three.

Cutting in (abklatschen) is only done at informal German parties.

Night Spots

Discrimination?

Some disco-type establishments use signs such as *"Privat-Club"* or *"Nur für Mitglieder"* (Members Only) to be able to handpick their patrons, especially on busy nights. A few are also known to discriminate against young foreign workers and soldiers. They claim that some of the young foreigners are troublemakers and that their noisy behavior will frighten away the steady German patrons, or that the way they are dressed does not fit the establishment.

It is true that in Germany owners have the right to deny entrance to their establishment, but only for a specific reason. If the customer is not at fault in any way, then it's a case of discrimination, and soldiers should report such cases to the commanders. They will take up action with the disco manager or with the appropriate German authorities who on the whole have proven very cooperative in such cases.

Often, however, it is hard to say whether the reason for turning away patrons really is discrimination or actual overcrowding.

Likewise, it is hard to distinguish between poor service and an intentional slight.

An American military paper gave wise advice to its readers: "Act in a European tavern in the same way you would want a foreign soldier to act in a tavern in your home town."

Theater Tickets

"Bitte zwei Karten zu ... Mark für die Acht-Uhr-Vorstellung!" (Two tickets, please, at ... marks, for the 8 o'clock show/performance), is about what one would say when buying tickets for the movie theater *(das Kino)*, the theater *(das Theater)* or the opera *(die Oper)* — *Kasse* means box-office. The word for booking in advance is *Vorverkauf.*

When buying tickets, one must know the difference in the seats. *Parkett* in German means orchestra, a *Loge* is a box, *1.* or *2. Rang* means first or second balcony, *Balkon* is usually the center part of the first balcony, and *Galerie* is the gallery. *"Reihe 7, Platz 10"* would mean 7th row, seat No. 10.

Germans dress up for the theater, concert and opera, but not for the movies.

Admission to movies is normally only between performances. No children under six are allowed in normal adult showings, and certain age groups are excluded from many other films under the German Youth Protection Law.

Leisure Time Pursuits

How do the Germans spend their leisure time? Opinion pollsters have provided us with some information in this respect, too.

In the evenings, most people apparently watch TV or read papers or magazines. Entertaining visitors in the home rates third. This apparently depends on the size of the home: the larger the house, the more often guests are welcomed.

Every fourth German regularly visits a neighborhood pub *(Stammlokal)* for a glass of beer or wine and a chat with friends.

Every third person in the 13 to 15 year-age group spends the leisure hours with a "clique" of ten or more, going in for sports, swimming, exchanging records, etc. Of the 16 to 18 year-olds, only 15 per cent visit a disco occasionally on weekends.

Cultural Activities

Because of its long tradition of particularism and cultural diversity, Germany has always been extremely rich in theaters, opera and concert houses, museums, and libraries, most of which are generously supported by state subsidies. In tiny West Germany alone, there are 300 theaters, 80 symphony orchestras, and 1,800 museums.

Actually, most Germans themselves do not even realize how well off they are in this respect. Every fifth citizen said he or she had never visited a theater, concert or museum.

The Outdoors

As for outdoor activities, walking, hiking, swimming and gardening are most popular.

Two thirds of all families go for a walk *(Spazierengehen)* regularly on Sundays. Many Germans still get out their best clothes on Sunday, but there is a strong tendency towards casual wear on holidays, especially among people who are tied to an office desk during the week and happy to get rid of formal clothes on the weekend.

Germans love gardening. More than half of all households have a garden to call their own. Everywhere you can see the carefully tended plots, often in colonies of *Kleingärten* or *Schrebergärten* with their standardized wooden huts. Green thumbs are not only active in gardens and backyards, but also on most balconies, and 92 per cent of households have potted plants.

If you like hiking through unspoiled country-side you have probably noticed triangular signs bearing the emblem of a large, flying bird and the word *Landschaftsschutzgebiet* or *Naturschutzgebiet*. These are "protected areas" or "natural reserves", with the latter meaning absolute protection of all plants and animals living in the area.

Other Hobbies

Sports, too, are an important leisure time pursuit, of course (see page 129). Other popular hobbies include collecting (an estimated eight million collectors of all sorts, including four million stamp collectors), choir singing, photography, wireless telegraphy, homing pigeons, etc.

Volksmarching

"Volksmarsch" (or *Volkswanderung, Volkswandertag)* is a German word for an organized hike or walk — there's no "marching" on a *Volksmarsch,* and no competition either. American soldiers stationed in Germany and their families have taken to the idea for several reasons: it's a good way to meet and get to know the German people; it's fun, and you get close to nature; and, finally, it's a healthful activity. Each weekend, many thousands of Americans participate in the *Volksmarsch* phenomenon.

Usually, a *Volksmarsch* leads along well marked trails in distances from five to 42 kilometers. Most marches have at least two distances (usually 10 and 20 km) and some have three or four (usually including a marathon hike of 30 km).

Besides improving their health, volksmarchers can also earn awards for each march in the form of certificates, plates, plaques or medals. For continued participation, pins and badges are awarded. Most Volksmarches are organized by groups such as IVV, EVG, DLV or DWB which conduct events throughout the year.

Every *Volksmarsch* is well publicized in the area. There are also many clubs you can join. Clubs offer a variety of volksmarching benefits, including preregistration.

A close relative of the volksmarch is the *"Volkslauf"* (run). *Volksläufe* are sponsored by the German Track and Field Federation and are timed events. The competition aspect of the *Volkslauf* is what differentiates it from the volksmarch.

On the Beach

Northern Germany has fine beach resorts. Bathing attire is about the same as in the States. Very small children, however, often swim and play on the beach naked (even many adults do in some areas).

Beach life German style entails renting a *Strandkorb* ("beach chair") or building for yourself a *Burg* (low circular wall of sand), but it is also usual to sun yourself while lying on a blanket. The *Strandkorb* and the *Burg* protect the bather from the wind.

Since adults don't usually run through the town in beach attire, they must obviously change someplace (bathing cabins are only known at public swimming pools). It's quite an art to get out of your suit and into your clothes in public with the aid of a protective *Bademantel* (bath robe, usually made from terry cloth). But that's the way it's done. Your neighbors, in the meantime, will discreetly look at the birds passing overhead or at an imaginary steamer in the distance.

The Weather

German weather is similar to the weather in the northern-central United States. There is plenty of rain in most places, so the "Tips for Coping with Hamburg's Weather", which an American woman published for the benefit of her compatriots living here, are valid for other German regions as well:

1. Accept the fact that it often rains in Hamburg (a drizzly, damp and continuous rain).

2. Never plan an outdoor event where success depends completely upon good weather. Always have an alternative idea in case of rain.

3. Never cancel plans because of rain or wait until a drizzle stops because you may find yourself postponing for days.

4. Voluntary isolation because of bad weather just makes a gray day grayer.

5. Armed with a rain coat (yellow with a hood!), an umbrella and rain boots, forge ahead — you'll notice Germans are all out in the wet and don't even seem to notice it.

6. Dress warmly — which may mean undershirts for the whole family.

7. Don't consider putting winter clothes into storage before May and then you may need to only pack heavy winter coats and boots.

8. Even sunny days can be cold because of the wind. A wind breaker with a hood (and zip-out warm lining for year-round use) is essential.

9. Birds awake chirping at 4 a. m., and may bother you in the summer. You'll probably go to work or send your children to school in the dark in winter.

10. Decorate rooms in bright, light colors. Add bright touches to dectract from outside gloom. Use cut flowers and candles.

Summer temperatures can get into the 90s — but seldom for more than a few days or weeks. In the winter the temperature is often below freezing. The coldest weather is in the Alps; Germany's warmest area is the Upper Rhine Valley, in the southwest.

The weather is much less extreme in Central Europe than in most parts of the U. S. The moderating influence of the western winds from the Atlantic Ocean is stronger than the hot or cold air streams coming from the eastern land masses. Intense heat is as rare as is extreme cold or blizzards. There are heavy storms at the coasts sometimes but nothing comparable to hurricanes. Earthquakes are practically unknown — apart from a very slight shake once in a while in the southwest or west of the country.

Geographically, Germany lies at the same latitude approximately as southern Canada. Summer days in Germany are longer than in the U. S., winter days are shorter. Summer and winter take long in coming: the spring and fall seasons stretch over longer periods than in more southern countries.

(Courtesy of the American Women's Club of Hamburg)

Soccer, Skat, and Bowling

"Fußball" (soccer) is the leading popular sport in Germany, comparable in its popularity only to U. S. baseball and football combined.

"Skat" is by far the most popular card game. All it takes is three players and a pack of 32 cards — but also a lot of practice.

"Kegeln" (nine-pins) is a bowling game — like ten-pins played without the headpin. Many Germans enjoy the cheerful companionship this game brings about.

The Popular Games

If you live in Germany and are looking for an opportunity to come into contact with Germans, joining a sports club may be a good idea: Almost one third of the German population are organized in 63,000 sports clubs of all sorts.

Soccer

Soccer *(Fußball)*, of course, is the king of sports in Germany — attracting an average of 20 million spectators both to the arenas and TV sets every Saturday afternoon during the *Bundesliga* season. The big championship matches and the European "Cups" and other international encounters draw up to 70 per cent of the German population to the TV sets.

The *Fußball-Bundesliga* (Federal Soccer League) is the "first division" of German soccer, consisting of the 18 best teams.

Every season two to three teams are "demoted" and two to three advance from the second into the first division.

It is not only the dramatic fight for the championship and the just as bitter fight against "demotion" that makes this sport so attractive but also the local patriotism involved, the stardom of the high-paid players and coaches and — last but not least — the game itself, the rules of which are easy to understand for everybody.

Other Sports Clubs

Next to soccer, athletics clubs *(Turnvereine)* have the most members. Rifle, track and field, tennis, swimming, handball, and table tennis clubs follow, in that order.

Kegeln

Nine-pin bowling *(Kegeln)*, a bowling game resembling ten-pins played without the headpin, is also very popular: three to four million Germans play it regularly.

U.S.-style bowling, too, has become very popular in Germany in recent decades.

Skat

The number of people playing *Skat*, the most popular card game in Germany, is about 20 million. It is a typical German institution and is played at all levels of society. Even the members of Bonn's parliament have their own club, and a large tavern there organizes a monthly tournament at which journalists and politicians oppose each other.

Contrary to *Fußball*, *Skat* rules are not so easily learned, and it takes a while to learn both the rules and the language of bidding and scoring. Once absorbed, however, it can become a fascinating game.

Appendix

Metric — U. S. Conversion

German Metric   **U. S.**

1	Gramm (g)	0.035	ounce
1	Pfund (500 Gramm)	1.1	pounds
1	Kilogramm	2.2	pounds
1	Zentimeter (cm)	0.3937	inch
2.54	Zentimeter	1	inch
1	Meter (m)	3.280	feet
1609.3	Meter	1	mile

Liquid Measure

1	Centiliter (cl)	0.338	fluidounce
1	Deciliter (dl)	0.21	pint
1	Liter (l)	2.113	pints
1	Liter	1.056	quarts
3.785	Liter	1	gallon

Dry Measure

1	Deciliter (dl)	0.18	pint
1	Liter	0.908	quart
1	Hektoliter (100 liters)	2.837	bushels

Kilometers — Miles

km	m
1	0.6
3	1.8
5	3.1
8	4.9
10	6.2
15	9.3
20	12.4
25	15.5
30	18.6
35	21.7
40	24.8
45	27.9
50	31.0
100	62.1
150	93.1
200	124.2
250	155.2
300	186.4
350	217.4
400	248.5
450	279.5
500	310.6

Kitchen Hints

U. S.	Europe
1 cup sugar	200 g
1 cup flour	150 g
1 tsp.	5 g
1 tbsp.	12 g
1 lb.	450 g
1 kilo	2.2 lb.

Do you get tired of always ordering Wiener Schnitzel in German restaurants because you don't know how to translate the menu? Here is a handy reference table to make it easy for you to know your way around. Clip it out and keep it in your wallet or purse. Guten Appetit!

Vorspeisen — Hors d'Oeuvres

Vorspeisen	Hors d'Oeuvres
Blätterteigpastete	(flaky) pastry
Forellenfilet	Fillet of smoked trout
Räucheraal	Smoked eel
Räucherlachs	Smoked salmon
Weinbergschnecken	Snails

Suppen — Soups

Suppen	Soups
Bohnensuppe	Bean soup
Champignonsuppe	Mushroom soup
Erbsensuppe	Pea soup
Gulaschsuppe	Hungarian soup
Hühnerbrühe	Chicken broth
Kraftbrühe	Broth
Linsensuppe	Lentil soup
Ochsenschwanzsuppe	Oxtail soup
Spargelcremesuppe	Asparagus soup
Tomatensuppe	Tomato soup

Salate — Salads

Salate	Salads
Gurkensalat	Cucumber salad
Gemischter Salat	Mixed salad
Kopfsalat	Lettuce salad
Tomatensalat	Tomato salad

Fische — Fish

Fische	Fish
Aal	Eel
Forelle	Trout
Hecht	Pike
Heilbutt	Halibut
Hering	Herring
Kabeljau	Cod
Karpfen	Carp
Krabben	Small Shrimps
Lachs	Salmon
Makrele	Mackerel
Matjes	Pickled herring
Muscheln	Mussels
Rotbarsch	Red Fish
Schellfisch	Fresh Haddock
Scholle	Plaice
Seezunge	Sole
Steinbutt	Turbot

Fleisch — Meat

Fleisch	Meat
Kalb	Veal
Lamm	Lamb
Rind/Ochsen-	Beef
Schweine-	Pork
Beefsteakhack	Ground beef
Braten	Roast
Bratwurst	Fried sausage
Eisbein	Pickled pork
Filetsteak	Fillet steak
Frikassee	Fricassee
Gulasch	Stewed steak cubes, gulyas
Haxe	Knuckle
Hirn	Brains
Kasseler (Rippchen)	Smoked ribs of pork
Keule	Leg of meat
Kotelett	Loin
Leber	Liver
Nieren	Kidneys
Ragout	Ragout/Stew
Rouladen	Rolled meat, braised
Rumpsteak	Rumpsteak
Steak	Beefsteak
Schinken	Ham
Soße	Sauce, Gravy
Wiener Schnitzel	Fillets of veal à la Viennoise (Breaded veal cutlet)

Geflügel — Poultry

Geflügel	Poultry
Ente	Duck
Gans (Gänsebraten)	Goose
Huhn/Hähnchen	Chicken
Puter	Turkey

Wild — Game

Wild	Game
Hase	Hare/Rabbit
Hirsch	Venison
Kaninchen	Rabbit
Reh	Roebuck
Rücken	Saddle
Wildschwein	Wild Boar

Eierspeisen — Egg Dishes

Eierspeisen	Egg Dishes
Pfannkuchen	German pancake
Rührei	Scrambled eggs
Spiegeleier	Fried eggs
Verlorene Eier	Poached eggs

Beilagen

Bratkartoffeln
Kartoffelbrei (Püree)
Knödel
Leberknödel
Nudeln
Pommes frites
Reis
Salzkartoffeln
Spätzle

Side Order

Fried potatoes
Mashed potatoes
Dumplings
Liver dumplings
Noodles
French fries
Rice
Boiled potatoes
Spätzle (dumplings)

Gemüse

Artischocken
Auberginen
Blumenkohl
Fenchel
Grüne Bohnen
Grüne Erbsen
Grünkohl
Gurke
Karotten, Möhren
Knoblauch
Linsen
Paprika
Pilze
Porree, Lauch
Rosenkohl
Rotkraut, -kohl
Sellerie
Spargel
Spinat
Staudensellerie
Tomaten
Weißkraut
Zwiebeln

Vegetables

Artichoke
Eggplant
Cauliflower
Fennel
Green beans
Green peas
Kale
Cucumber
Carrots
Garlic
Lentils
Sweet pepper
Mushrooms
Leek
Brussels Sprouts
Red cabbage
Celeriac
Asparagus
Spinach
Celery
Tomatoes
White cabbage
Onions

Früchte

Apfel
Apfelsine, Orange
Birne
Erdbeeren
Himbeeren
Johannisbeeren
Kirschen
Pfirsich
Zitrone
Zwetsche

Fruits

Apple
Orange
Pear
Strawberries
Rasperries
Currants
Cherries
Peach
Lemon
Damson

Zubereitungsarten

blau (Fisch)
gebacken
gebraten
gedünstet
gefüllt
gekocht
geschmort
in Backteig
mit Butter
paniert
mit Remouladensauce
vom Rost/gegrillt
mit Schlagsahne

Preparation

blue (fish boiled)
baked/fried
roasted/fried
steamed
stuffed
boiled
braised/stewed
in batter
with butter
with breadcrumbs
with remoulade sauce
grilled, broiled
with whipped cream

Kalte Speisen

Aufschnitt
Käseplatte
Schinken
(roh/gekocht)

Cold Dishes

Cold cuts
Assorted cheeses
Ham
(smoked/boiled)

Nachtisch

Eis
Kompott
Obst, frisches
Obstsalat
Rote Grütze

Gebäck

Berliner Pfannkuchen

Blätterteiggebäck

Kekse
Obstkuchen
Sandkuchen
Teegebäck
Torte

Getränke

Bier (hell/dunkel)
Liköre/Spirituosen

Rotwein
Sekt
Süßwein
Weinbrand
Weißwein
Limonade
Mineralwasser
Saft

Dessert

Ice cream
Stewed fruit
Fresh fruit
Fruit salad
Red berry pudding

Pastry

Berlin doughnuts
(Bismarcks)
Puff pastry (turn-
overs, tarts)
Cookies
Fruit cake
Pound cake
Tea cakes
Layered cake
(often very rich)

Beverages

Beer (pale/dark)
Liqueurs/spirits
(liquors)
Red wine
German Champagne
Dessert wine
Brandy
White wine
Lemonade
Mineralwater
Juice

Clothes Sizes U.S. — Europe

Skirts, Dresses, Coats

U.S.	Europe
10	38
12	40
14	42
16	44
18	46
20	48

Suits

U. S.	Europe
36	46
38	48
40	50
42	52
44	54
46	56
48	58

Shirts

U.S.	Europe
14	36
14 1/2	37
15	38
15 1/2	39
16	41
16 1/2	42
17	43

Blouses

U. S.	Europe
30	38
32	40
34	42
36	44
38	46
40	48

Shoes

U.S.	Europe
6	37
7	38
8	39
9	40
10	41
11	42
12	43
13	44

Hats

U. S.	German
7 1/8	57
7 1/4	58
7 3/8	59
7 1/2	60
7 5/8	61

Here are some tips for easy conversion of U. S. clothes sizes to German sizes:

For blouses, add 8 to your U. S. size to get the German size, for example, if you wear a 34 U. S., you'll take a 42 German. For dresses and skirts you'll have to add 28 to your U. S. size. For shoes, you add 31. For example, size six would become size 37.

Thermometer Readings

German thermometers use the centigrade scale. To convert Fahrenheit to centigrade, subtract 32, then multiply by 5 and divide by 9. To convert centigrade to Fahrenheit, multiply by 9, divide by 5 and add 32. Chart below gives approximate conversion.

C	F
38	100.4
35	95
30	86
25	77
21	69.8
10	50
5	41
0	32
— 5	23
— 10	14
— 15	5
— 17	1.4
— 25	— 13
— 30	— 22

Index

**Other
Atlantik-Brücke
Publications:**

**Meet Germany
German Holidays and Folk Customs
Meeting German Business
German Place Names**